Subversive Wisdom

Subversive Wisdom

Sociopolitical Dimensions of John's Gospel

BERT NEWTON

WIPF & STOCK · Eugene, Oregon

SUBVERSIVE WISDOM
Sociopolitical Dimensions of John's Gospel

Wipf & Stock
An imprint of Wipf and Stock Publishers
199 W. 8th Ave., Suite 3
Eugene, OR 97401

www.wipfandstock.com

ISBN 13: 978-1-61097-822-4

Manufactured in the U.S.A.

To my wife, Gloria, my companion in the countercultural wisdom journey

. . . God chose what is foolish in the world to shame the wise; God chose what is weak in the world to shame the strong; God chose what is low and despised in the world, things that are not, to reduce to nothing things that are . . . (1 Cor 1:27–28, NRSV)

Contents

Foreword

JOHN'S GOSPEL IS OFTEN THOUGHT TO PRESENT A JESUS THAT IS so exalted as to be almost floating in the heavens. In this refreshing commentary, Bert Newton clarifies our vision by offering us a more accurate image of the Johannine Jesus, as Wisdom walking (and talking!) on the earth. Newton even suggests that we might dare to follow those first-century Jewish Galilean footsteps down our own city streets.

The evocative image of Wisdom walking grows organically out of Bert's own life of down-to-earth discipleship. His feet are quite firmly planted (if always ready to move!) on the streets of Pasadena and around the greater Los Angeles metropolis. My wife and I had the privilege of walking with Bert for five years, living just two blocks away. I offer here a few "street-level" snapshots of the commitments and context that shape Bert's daily walk in the way of Jesus and thus informed the writing of this book.

Bert's day job of many years entails walking alongside folks in transition, often out of LA's "prison-industrial complex." It has been estimated that the institution housing the greatest number of mentally ill people in the country is actually the LA County jail system! His daily grind as a mental health case manager and housing specialist includes assisting and advocating for people as they seek stable housing, jobs, counseling, sobriety, dignity, and restoration to full status as citizens in a caring community. Just as the heart of Jesus' ministry revolved around restoring outcasts and the "lost sheep of Israel" to their rightful status as beloved sons and daughters of Abraham, Bert befriends folks struggling to overcome many obstacles to inclusion in our society. Bert even risked his own employment by providing leadership in an attempt to unionize his organization's staff, so his concern for justice extends beyond his clients to his coworkers. And in keeping with his "act local" orientation (and our itinerant imagery), Bert usually walks to work, a rare phenomenon in LA!

Bert has also walked for many years with a local body of Christ followers called Pasadena Mennonite Church, where he has been a "pillar" of the church, including serving it for a decade as an (unpaid) pastor with an MDiv degree from nearby Fuller Theological Seminary. My wife Jennifer learned much from Bert about witnessing to the way of Jesus during her five years on the pastoral team at PMC, a small yet special congregation of individuals who, like Bert, bring the best of their often evangelical (and/or Reformed backgrounds) into their chosen spiritual stream of the Anabaptist tradition.

One creative witness to peace and justice in Jesus' way that grew out of this faith community and Bert's pastoral leadership (originally in response to the US invasion of Iraq in 2003) literally involves walking: the (now annual and still growing) Pasadena Palm Sunday Peace Parade! Walking joyfully from the margins of Pasadena to its centers of power (City Hall and the Paseo Colorado shopping "temple"), an ecumenical mix of local congregations, families, and people of goodwill annually recreates Jesus' wisdom walk into the center of power in his society, the capital city, temple cult, and Roman fortress that was first-century Jerusalem ("riding a donkey, not a warhorse," as one perennially popular Peace Parade sign proclaims). This ancient-yet-new Holy Week tradition has now spread to other communities around the country via the Mennonite Church network. My pastor-wife took it with us to our new church home in Virginia.

Bert also walks in the wise way of Jesus in a daily manner in his neighborhood, living in intentional community with the "Urban Village." Bert and his artist-with-a-social-consciousness wife Gloria are founding members and (youngish!) "elders" of this decade-old motley crew of Jesus-walkers, who live mostly on the same block and share a life of discipleship together via mutual aid to each other, hospitality to strangers, studying the Word, front yard firepits, and incubating creative ideas for social change in their community. For example, one long-term member of the Urban Village—with the support of the whole group—was instrumental in starting up the Pasadena "Peace and Justice Academy," which seeks to shape a new generation of middle and high schoolers in the wisdom walking ways of Jesus.

I once got arrested with Bert and spent an interesting overnight in an LA jail along with hundreds of others in one of the largest civil disobedience actions in the city's history (part of a longer-term and ultimately successful "living wage" campaign for mostly immigrant women working in the LAX hotel industry). So I wasn't surprised to receive recent emailed reports of Bert's active involvement in the "Occupy Pasadena" movement. That's just the kind of guy Bert is.

Woven through all these commitments (and others) is Bert's dynamic gifts as a teacher of the Bible. Bert has a special ability to bring together "the sanctuary, the seminary, and the street" (to quote his California collaborators in Christ, Ched Myers and Elaine Enns). Along with many of us, he is energized by the process of continually uncovering and recapturing the spirit of the original messianic movement for radical renewal that formed around Jesus. This book represents some of the best fruit of many years of Bert's "working with the Word." Bert's Bible teaching, organizing skills, and—above all else—his authentic friendship in Christ has certainly encouraged and empowered my small steps "walking in the way" of God's Wisdom-Word: Jesus of Nazareth. I trust this book will do the same for you, if you but "take and read!"

Kent Davis Sensenig
Harrisonburg, VA
January 1, 2012

Preface

I HAD A FRIEND IN COLLEGE NAMED TIM. TIM WAS BIG. HE transferred into our college from another where he had played offensive line for the football team. Tim had two older brothers who were even bigger than he was; one of them had played offensive line for the Houston Oilers.

Tim told me that, while traveling through Georgia one time, his two older brothers stopped for breakfast at a restaurant where a sign in the window said, "All the pancakes you can eat for 99 cents!" So his two brothers went in and ordered the pancakes. After they polished off the first stack, they ordered more . . . and then more . . . and then more, until finally the waitress told them that they could not have any more pancakes. Surprised that she would so blatantly contradict the restaurant's advertising, they exclaimed, "But the sign says, 'All the pancakes you can eat for 99 cents!'" Without missing a beat, the waitress replied, "That *is* all the pancakes you can eat for 99 cents!"

The moral of this story: There is always another way to read the text.

READING THE BIBLICAL TEXT

Probably the most interpreted and reinterpreted text in the world is the Bible. This holy text has given rise to a wide range of readings. For some, this book blesses hierarchies and imperial war. For others it teaches nonviolence and justice for the poor. At one level, the Bible functions much like a Rorschach test: what we see in it, what we choose to learn from it, says more about us than what is actually in the text itself. This text, then, functions two ways: we can read it, and it can read us.

In Luke 10:25–28, Jesus seems to be using this dialectical dynamic of the biblical text when responding to a question about salvation. A teacher of the Torah asks him, "What must I do to inherit eternal life?" Jesus answers his question with a question, "What does the Torah say, how do you read it?" In other words, the man's salvation depends not merely on what the text says, but *how* the man *reads* the text. How the man reads the text will reveal whether he has allowed the text to read him, whether he has allowed the word of God to enter into him to transform him.

I think that Jesus, were he around today in the flesh, might put the same question to us: How do we read the Scriptures? The way that we answer that question will reveal much about us.

In Jesus' interaction with the teacher of the Torah, the stress falls on loving one's neighbor. The teacher first recites the two greatest commandments of Torah, to love God and to love one's neighbor, but it is the second one that causes the problem and leads Jesus to tell the parable of the Good Samaritan.

It is that second commandment that always causes the problem. The first one is easy, because without the second commandment to give it flesh, we can play it out any way we like. We can make God personal and private, or we can make God bless whatever we do, or we can make God the purveyor of feel-good religion. It is that second commandment that grounds us and makes us accountable. It is in that second commandment that the word of God becomes "living and active, sharper than a two-edged sword, piercing until it divides soul from spirit, joints from marrow, able to judge the thoughts and intentions of the heart"(Heb 4:12, NRSV). That second commandment reads us like a book.

Reading the Bible politically means reading the text through the lens of that second commandment. A political reading of

Scripture allows no ungrounded piety but rather demands that piety be grounded in the real world where people live, work, suffer, love, hope, and die. A political reading gives attention to human social relationships and power dynamics that ungrounded piety often ignores. A political reading requires brutal honesty and openness on the part of the reader, or more accurately, on the part of the reading community.

People do not read the Bible all alone but always as part of a larger interpretive community. Even when reading in private, the assumptions and biases of the reader's wider community influence the way the material is understood. If that interpretive community does not put much stress on that second commandment, it may promote a reading of the biblical text that ignores social and power dynamics and interpret the text apolitically or even as blessing top-down, authoritarian social structures. Lately, some popular right wing commentators have even found in the Bible wholehearted support for free market capitalism.

Since the North American church is one of those interpretive communities that tends strongly toward readings of the Bible that do not use the commandment to love one's neighbor as an interpretive lens, extra effort has to be made to help us read the Bible politically. People like Ched Myers, Walter Wink, and Richard Horsley have helped me tremendously in this regard. I do not pretend to have reached anywhere near their heights of exegetical analysis and insight, but this book is my humble attempt to help others in the same way.

A NOTE ABOUT JOHN'S ISRAELITE CHARACTER

Having completed the main body of my book, I began to have various people read my manuscript for feedback. One of my readers registered a strong, but polite, objection to the "supersessionism" of my argument, i.e., that I had read John as promoting the new community of Jesus followers, the church, to be the new Israel, the replacement of the old Israel, thereby implicitly negating the Jewish people. As I took another look at my manuscript in the light of this critique, I was shocked to find out that my critic was right about the supersessionism (but not about negating the Jewish people, as I will explain below). Although I had long ago developed an understanding of the gospels and Jesus as thoroughly Israelite, I had just written a book that interpreted the message of the Fourth Gospel as proclaiming the church to be Israel's replacement.

Working through my manuscript again, however, I found that my conclusion was inescapable. John's gospel was written in the wake of the destruction of Israel and its temple, and it proclaims the rebirth of Israel through Jesus' death and resurrection, emerging as the transnational community of Jesus followers. There are a few qualifications, however, that need to be noted.

The message of John's gospel, as well as the community that produced it, remains thoroughly Israelite. The proclamation of John's gospel is, therefore, that of a marginalized minority voice with in a larger dominant community. Through this gospel, this marginalized minority appeals to the egalitarian traditions found in the Torah and Israel's prophetic and wisdom writings. Its polemic should be understood in this context, much like a contemporary harsh critique of the American political establishment by a radical group in the United States that uses the rhetoric of reclaiming the founding ideals of American democracy to recreate the nation so that it can be a beacon of democracy for the whole world and even transcend nationalism in solidarity with freedom-loving people everywhere.

John's message was later misused by a church that had become largely gentile and whose leadership proved to be not only anti-Semitic but also diametrically opposed to the Gospel's message of equality, justice, and nonviolence. This church used John's "supersessionist" message as justification for its anti-Semitic policies and teachings. The Israelite community that produced John's gospel could not have foreseen this development. This community believed that their message was *the way* that Israel would survive, grow stronger, enfold the gentiles, and defeat the Roman Empire.

The Fourth Gospel's constant allusion and reference to Israel's scriptures and history—virtually every sentence in the text is formed by and pays tribute to its Israelite heritage—and its report that Jesus told the Samaritan woman, "Salvation is from the Judeans," reflect its allegiance to Israel. The community that proclaimed this gospel firmly believed itself to be more faithful to God's vision for Israel than the wider Judean/Israelite Diaspora community.

Acknowledgments

I AM GREATLY INDEBTED TO ALL THE PEOPLE WHO HELPED ME write this book by reading the manuscript and giving me their feedback: Ched Myers, Wes Howard-Brook, Warren Carter, Joe Roos, Joe Bautista, Kent Sensenig, Jennifer Davis Sensenig, Gloria Newton, David Martyn, and Melissa Hofstetter.

1

The Message of John's Gospel

THE GOSPEL OF JOHN TELLS THE STORY OF A COUNTERCUL-
ture Messiah who embodies the subversive wisdom of God
and, through his death and resurrection, *drives out* "the ruler of
this world." The culture that he counters is not so much the culture
of the people as it is the culture of the rulers, a culture that the
rulers impose upon the people. "The ruler of this world" whom
he drives out is the spirit of domination and empire, the spirit that
inhabits all oppressive systems. The victory of this Messiah is both
final, completed in his crucifixion and resurrection, and continues to be realized by all who follow after and believe in him; they
continue, through the way of the cross, the battle to "drive out the
ruler of this world."

WHAT!?

The above description of the Gospel of John does not reflect the
prevailing interpretation, either among scholars or lay readers,
of this gospel. The Bible, in general, in modern times tends to be
interpreted apolitically. This mode of interpretation holds even
more firmly in New Testament interpretation and, among the four
canonical gospels, finds its apex in the Gospel of John, often called

"the spiritual gospel." The prevailing apolitical interpretations of the Gospel of John and the rest of the Bible, however, arise out of the virtually complete dichotomy between faith/spirituality/religion and sociopolitical realities that holds sway in modern Western culture, a dichotomy not shared by the ancient cultures that produced the Bible. The ancient world knew no separation between temple and state, much less between faith and politics.

However beneficial the separation between church and state may be in modern Western societies, the further separation of faith and politics (a separation that our culture can never completely sustain, as demonstrated especially by U.S. presidential elections) has crippled our culture's ability to understand its most widely read religious text as well as its ability to read the deeper spiritual subtext of its own political narrative. One of the few interpreters of the Gospel of John who has explored its political dimensions, Wes Howard-Brook, comes to the following conclusion:

> What the narrator of the fourth gospel makes crystal clear is that religion and politics are, in the end, the same thing. Both claim the availability of ultimate power to shape people's lives. The only question for either is whether the power is claimed of life or of death, of God or of Satan.[1]

Whether or not one is ready to accept the idea that, even in today's world, political matters are ultimately religious/spiritual and that religious/spiritual matters are ultimately political, this worldview does hold true for the authors and original audiences of the Bible. The Gospel of John tells a story that is both religious/spiritual and sociopolitical. Like the rest of the Bible, the text does not distinguish between the political and religious dimensions of life.

With this insight, this book will attempt to trace the contours of John's political message, the good news of the subversive wisdom of the way of the cross.

---

1. Howard-Brook, *Becoming Children*, 374.

JESUS IS GOD!

For some pious, modern readers of the Gospel of John, its emphasis on the divinity of Jesus, what has been called its "high Christology," comprises a major, if not *the* major, teaching of this gospel, and not without reason. The text begins by declaring, "In the beginning was the word, and the word was with God, and the word *was* God . . . and the word became flesh and dwelt among us." Later, in 8:58, Jesus declares his identity using the name that God uses to self-identify in Exodus 3:14: ". . . before Abraham was, I am!" Jesus uses "I am" statements 19 other times in the story to speak of himself: 4:26, 6:35, 6:41, 6:48, 6:51, 8:12, 8:23, 8:24, 8:28, 9:5, 10:11, 10:30, 10:36, 10:38, 11:25, 13:19, 14:6, 15:1, 18:5, and 18:8. One additional statement would be an "I am" statement except that the verb is plural: Jesus announces in 10:30, "I and the Father are one," combining the force of an "I am" statement with a clear declaration of his unity with the Father. Jesus follows up this declaration in 14:9 with the explanation, "Whoever has seen me has seen the Father." The divinity of Jesus, then, certainly comprises a major theme in the book. The question remains, however, whether this theme constitutes an end in itself or serves a more specific purpose for the original readers of the book.

JOHN'S PURPOSE

Consideration of the original context in which the Gospel of John was written, along with a literary unpacking of its themes, reveals that this gospel aims to do more than make mere theological statements. The Gospel of John speaks to a context in which the temptation to accommodate to the ways of the world runs high, and this gospel attempts to convince its readers/hearers to persevere in the way of the cross, a way, or wisdom, that runs counter to the ways of the world.

The Gospel of John addresses a primarily Judean[2] audience living in Ephesus in the late first to the early second centuries CE. Beyond that consensus, the makeup of the audience is much debated among scholars, but the possibilities allow for a range of people who can be placed along a spectrum of relationship to the community of Jesus-followers that produced this gospel, from committed followers of Jesus to people who are only considering becoming disciples to enemies of the community. The text itself provides clues as to the possible makeup of this audience: In the story, Jesus engages people who have committed to following him but nonetheless need comfort and reassurance as well as challenge (chapters 13–17), people who began following but whose commitment proves inadequate as Jesus' message becomes clearer (6:66,

---

2. The term "Judean(s)" is employed in this book rather than the term "Jew(s)" because many scholars now believe that the term *Ioudaioi* denotes people either from Judea or having an allegiance to the political entity of Judea, rather than people whom we would think of today as "Jews" due to their ethnicity or religion. In this way of thinking, the term "Jew" is not an appropriate term until the third century when the Mishnah had been put into writing, the rebuilding of the temple had become a distant hope, and Rabbinic Judaism had fully emerged as a religion that could be practiced with little or no connection to the temple or to the land of Palestine.

In John, the term seems mostly to denote those with a political or ideological allegiance to the religo-political establishment in Jerusalem, which before 70 CE ruled from the temple mount and after 70 CE survived through the Pharisaic movement that eventually gave rise to Rabbinic Judaism. John, as well as the other canonical gospels, charges this establishment with being co-opted by Rome, although certain segments or members, such as Nicodemus, are seen as breaking away from the establishment in sympathy with the movement of those who follow Jesus. Jesus and his disciples are understood to be Israelites, coming from the land of Judah, and therefore sharing ethnicity and, to a large extent, the faith, of the Judeans, even understanding themselves, at a certain level, as "Judean." John has Jesus say to the Samaritan woman, "Salvation comes from the Judeans" (4:22). The term "Judean" in John, as well as in other literature of this period, must be understood in context. It can refer to a political-ideological allegiance, being from Judah as opposed to Galilee or some other part of Israel, or some other shade of meaning. See Hanson and Oakman, *Palestine in the Time of Jesus*, 162 for a discussion of the various contextual meanings of the term "Judean."

8:31–59), people who continue to seek after Jesus but are afraid to make a public commitment (Nicodemus, 3:1–9, 7:50–1, 19:39; Joseph of Arimathea, 19:38), as well as outright enemies who "persecute" him (5:16), fear the empire more than God (11:47–53, 19:15) expel from the synagogue those who follow him (9:22, 12:42, 16:2), and repeatedly attempt to arrest and/or kill him (5:18, 7:30, 32, 44, 8:59, 10:39, 18:1–14). These characters may reflect the various sorts of people that this gospel sought to engage at the time of its writing (as well as the types of people whom Jesus actually did engage).

The two groups that the Gospel of John seems to seek to engage the most are the committed faithful, as evidenced by the length of space given over to addressing them (chapters 13–17), and those on the fence, especially the ones hesitant to make a public commitment, as evidenced by the dialogue with Nicodemus in chapter 3 and the continued depiction of Nicodemus, and later Joseph of Arimathea, as "secret disciples." In addressing these two groups plus any others, the way the gospel describes Jesus becomes an integral part of the argument. Jesus has to be able to defeat the powers and authorities of this world in a way that appeals to Torah-believing Judeans, some of whom may be tempted to give up resistance. The "high Christology" of the narrative serves that purpose.

In the aftermath of the destruction of the temple, and virtually of Israel, by Rome, Judeans turned to the Torah for life and salvation. The Gospel of John presents Jesus as an even greater Torah, the Word and Wisdom of God, existing prior to the written Torah. In John, this eternal Word becomes a subversive Wisdom, a subversive Torah, which brings down the empire and "drives out the ruler of this world."

The propaganda of the Roman Empire proclaimed the emperor to be divine, "son of God," "savior of the world," one who "wipes away our sins," and "shepherd of the people." The Gospel of John (and the rest of the New Testament) claims these titles for

Jesus, displacing the emperor from his throne. In doing so, the narrative of John not only usurps these titles for Jesus but claims even more for Jesus than the imperial propaganda claimed for the emperor. John proclaims that Jesus is the "only" son of God (1:14, 18; 3:16, 18) and, in fact, *is* God, not just one of many gods. The Roman senate declared certain emperors to ascend to the gods after death, but the Gospel of John declares that only Jesus has ascended (3:13). In making these claims for Jesus, the Gospel of John and the rest of the New Testament proclaim that God is found at the bottom of the empire/world, not at the top, that salvation and liberation come from below, not from above (although, as we will see, John reverses the world order via a "heavenly" perspective, emphasizing that Jesus is "from above"), from a Galilean peasant with no citizenship in the empire rather than from the emperor. In John, Jesus not only displaces the emperor and turns the world upside down, his salvation proves greater and more substantial than that of the empire; he provides the truly "abundant life" (10:10).

SEEING THE UNSEEN

The evidence of Jesus' victory over the powers and authorities of this world, however, proves exceedingly difficult to see for the original readers of this text. They live in a context where the empire seems to remain dominant and victorious over all of its enemies, including the crucified Jesus of Nazareth. This gospel must somehow convince its readers of what they cannot see. It must convince them that the way of the cross is the way to life, that prophetic witness and martyrdom will in the end defeat the kingdoms of this world that conquer and maintain their rule by the sword. It must convince them that the dominant propaganda, the imperial culture around them, is a lie and that the counterculture way of Jesus is the truth—in other words, that Jesus is "the way, the truth and the life" (14:6).

The way of the cross in John (and the rest of the New Testament) finds its highest expression in martyrdom, but does not always include martyrdom for every person. The way of the cross more generally is the way of life that runs counter to the ways of the world, to the culture of empire and domination. According to John, the abundance of the world/empire is not true abundance, the life that it provides is actually death, and its hierarchy sustains its oppressive rule and must be abandoned and destroyed. In contrast, God's reign of peace and justice, where everyone submits to one another as equals, washing each other's feet, and where the poor are cleansed and fed, provides true abundance of life. The Gospel of John aims to help its readers see this unseen reign of God.

THE REST OF THIS BOOK

The rest of this book expands on the themes above in the following manner:

Chapter 2, "Against Empire," unpacks some terms and concepts in John's gospel, such as "eternal life" and "Son of Man," showing that these terms are both political and religious, further demonstrating that this gospel tells a story that is both sociopolitical and spiritual.

Chapter 3, "From God's Point of View," addresses the peculiar way in which this gospel is written, especially the peculiar portrayal of Jesus, so different from the other canonical gospels. In those gospels, Jesus appears as a Palestinian Judean peasant sage, telling kingdom parables. The Gospel of John portrays Jesus as a sort of Hellenistic Judean philosopher, speaking in long philosophical discourses about the concepts of "love" and "light" and "truth." This unique portrait of Jesus in John arises from this gospel's perspective: The Gospel of John tells the story of Jesus from a "heavenly" (3:12) perspective, from God's point of view. From that perspective, Jesus is not a mere human being but rather the personification of God's Word/Wisdom, a wisdom that runs counter to the world's wisdom; Jesus is God's Word/Wisdom walking around and talking, and he creates a new community of people who hear and live out his counterculture wisdom; they become a counterculture community whose ethos, the way of the cross, is only comprehensible from a "heavenly" perspective.

Chapter 4, "Israel Reborn," following up on the new community idea in John, unpacks the symbolism of the first three chapters of John, in which Jesus begins his ministry and calls together his disciple community. "Israel Reborn" shows that this new counterculture community is actually Israel reborn into the transnational kingdom of God.

Chapter 5, "Jesus is Torah," further emphasizes the Israelite theme by arguing that John's text not only portrays Jesus as God's Word/Wisdom but also as the incarnation of Torah. John presents Jesus in a way that appeals to Judeans who, after the fall of Jerusalem, have only the Torah to cling to for hope and salvation.

Chapter 6, "New Exodus," continues the Israelite theme, exploring the New Exodus motif in John: Jesus, like Moses, leads his people out from under bondage to the empire via the way of the cross to rebirth as the transnational kingdom of God.

Chapter 7, "Wisdom's Assault," returns to the theme of Jesus-as-Word/Wisdom, suggesting an overall plot summary for the Gospel of John: Acting and speaking according to God's countercultural wisdom, Jesus constantly behaves in ways contrary to expectations and frustrates his opponents. He is a sort of trickster, and his ultimate trick is to defeat the empire through allowing it to crucify him.

Chapter 8, "Life After Jesus," examines the last two chapters of John, suggesting that the stories of these two final chapters are included in the gospel to help the original audience, especially the believing audience, to believe in the victory of Jesus over the world despite all apparent evidence to the contrary. These passages help believers to "see" what is unseen and to follow in the way of the cross.

2

Against Empire

THE GOSPEL OF JOHN PRESENTS JESUS AND THE COMMUNITY that he founds as a new transnational Israel, the nation of Israel reborn into the kingdom of God, embarking on a new exodus of defection from the society around it that is the Roman Empire (chapters 4 and 6 of this book will examine this idea in the text of John). Much of the language of the Fourth Gospel, as well as of the whole NT, that appears to most modern readers as mere religious language is actually politically loaded, much of it directly challenging the Roman Empire. The ancient world did not know the sharp distinction between religious language and concepts and those of the sociopolitical realm that modern western readers tend to assume; in their world, religion and politics were inextricably intertwined; religious and political rulers where often the same people; religious and political institutions and rituals were often one and the same as well. Their language and concepts, therefore, would not have distinguished very much between the two realms. This chapter will examine some of the terms and concepts in the Gospel of John, most of them shared with the rest of the NT, which modern western readers tend to assume are politically neutral but that actually defy the Roman Empire.

9

JESUS USURPS THE THRONE OF CAESAR

The Gospel of John, like the other gospels, employs designations for Jesus that challenge the Roman emperor by stealing his honorary titles, thus supplanting him. The imperial propaganda referred to the emperor as "Son of God," "Savior of the world," "Shepherd," and even as the one who "wipes away our sins." For example (these references are plentiful), one inscription from Myra reads, "Divine Augustus Caesar, Son of God . . . Benefactor and Savior of the whole world . . ."[1] Another inscription from Ephesus proclaims Domition to be "Son of God Vespasian."[2] Dio Chrysostom reminds Trajan that the emperor should be a "Shepherd of peoples" who should "protect flocks."[3] Horace sings of Augustus, "Thine age, O Caesar, has brought back fertile crops to the fields . . . has wiped away our sins and revived the ancient virtues . . ."[4] By attributing these titles and roles to Jesus, John's gospel proclaims that Jesus, not the Roman emperor, is the true "Son of God," the real "Savior of the World," and "Shepherd" of the people—the one who actually takes away the sins of the common poor.

The context of the imperial propaganda, however, does not constitute the only source of meaning for these designations for Jesus in John. These terms also draw on Israelite tradition. The ideas of "Son of God," "Savior," "Shepherd," and the remission of sins carry sociopolitical meaning in the Hebrew Scriptures just as they did in the Greco-Roman world of the first century.

The Hebrew Scriptures employ the title "Savior" for God when speaking of God's acts of delivering Israel from foreign aggressors, especially empires (e.g., Isa 45:15, 21; Ps 78:9; 1 Macc 4:30). The term "shepherd" is used to refer to national human leaders (Num 27:17, Isa 44:28, Jer 43:12, Ezek 34:1–10) as well as

---

1. Braund, *Augustus to Nero*, 40.
2. Carter, *John and Empire*, 194.
3. Ibid., 186.
4. Odes 4.15, in Evans, *Bible Knowledge*, 187–88.

to God as leader of the nation (Ps 80:1, Ezek 34:11–15), often in contexts of God's deliverance of Israel from imperial domination (Jer 31:10, Isa 40:11). Jesus fulfills these roles from the Hebrew Scriptures while usurping them from the emperors.

The forgiveness of sins, while conceptualized today as a completely individual matter, in ancient Israel constituted a fundamental sociopolitical reality. Without forgiveness of sins, people could not fully participate in the social and economic life of their society because they would be considered unclean and, therefore, denied access to the centers of economic and social life. Furthermore, Israel understood its current domination by a foreign empire as punishment for its sin. Deliverance from sin meant deliverance from social and economic exclusion for the common poor and deliverance from foreign occupation and oppression for the nation.

The idea of God's son(s) occurs in various contexts in the Hebrew Scriptures with various meanings, including the Messiah (*4 Ezra* 7:28–29), the king of Israel (Ps 2:7) a persecuted righteous person who is vindicated by God (Wis 2:18), heavenly beings (Gen 6:4, Ps 89:6), and the collective people of Israel (Hos 11:1). Jesus, in John, fulfills all of these roles: He is the Messiah (Christ; 1:17, 2:41, 20:31), the king of Israel (1:49), a persecuted righteous person (7:19, 10:31, 15:22–25), a heavenly being (1:1–2), and the embodiment of his people. (He repeatedly refers to himself as the Son of Man, a collective image for Israel in Daniel 7; he also calls himself the "vine," in 15:1–8, which is an image for Israel in the Hebrew Scriptures.[5])

Jesus, in John, fulfills the roles of "Son of God" in the Hebrew Scriptures while subverting the "son of (a) god" mythology of the empire. The Roman propaganda proclaims the emperors to be sons of gods, to which the Gospel of John emphatically

5. Ps 80:8–16; Isa 5:1–7; Jer 2:21; Ezek 15:1–8, 17:1–10; Hos 10:1–2. Coins minted during the Maccabean period displayed a vine to symbolize Israel. Josephus records that the space above the entrance to the holy place in the temple displayed a golden vine symbolizing Israel (Evans, *Bible Knowledge*, 131).

retorts that Jesus is the "only" Son of God (1:14, 18; 3:16). In an ironic rhetorical twist, however, the gospel challenges the imperial mythology and propaganda in the other direction: Jesus is the "only" son of God, but he gives power to many to become "children of God" (1:12). Jesus both undercuts the divine status of the emperors through his uniqueness and simultaneously democratizes the world by giving everyone, potentially, the status that the emperors falsely claim for themselves.

THE SON OF MAN

The term "Son of Man" appears thirteen times in the Gospel of John. This title for Jesus derives from Daniel 7,[6] where "one like the son of man" is a collective image for the people of Israel as they overcome the empires that have ruled over them. By taking on this title, Jesus embodies his people, Israel, in its struggle against and ultimate triumph over the empire. In the vision of Daniel 7, four beasts represent four successive empires (or kingdoms) that rule over and oppress Israel. In contrast to these beasts, "one like the son of man," i.e., a human being, arrives from the heavens. God takes authority and power from the beasts and gives it to the human being. The interpretation of the vision in the latter part of the chapter identifies this human being as "the people of the holy ones of the most high," i.e., Israel (7:27).[7] Jesus, in John, brings the "son

6. The title "Son of Man" in the gospels seems to come primarily from Daniel 7, but also from 1 Enoch 37–71. Passages from the Wisdom of Solomon, 4 Ezra, and the Servant Songs of Isaiah, also serve as background for this title and what it conveys, without actually using the title. (More thorough discussions of this title can be found in Carter, John and Empire, 183–5 and in Nickelsburg, "Son of Man," 137–50.) Matt 24:30, 26:64, Mark 13:26, 14:62, and Luke 21:27 speak of the Son of Man "coming on the clouds" with "power" and "glory." Similarly, Daniel 7:13–14 tells of "one like the son of man coming on the clouds" and receiving "power and glory and kingship." Jesus first speaks of himself as "the Son of Man" in John when he tells Nathanael that he "will see heaven opened" (2:51), and John 5:27 states that Jesus will receive "power . . . because he is the Son of Man."

7. Nickelsburg suggests that "one like the son of man" in Daniel 7 is a

of man" metaphor of Daniel 7 to life, coming down from heaven (3:13, 31; 5:33–35; 8:23, 42), embodying his people,[8] receiving his authority from God (3:35; 5:22, 27), and triumphing over the empire (12:31–32; 16:33).

MESSIAH

Modern Christians typically assume that, while the Judeans of the first century hoped for a messiah who would liberate them from Roman rule, Jesus surprised them by being an apolitical messiah who saved individuals from their sins. This interpretation, however, stems from the general belief that the Gospel proclaims an apolitical message. The evidence presented in this study overturns that notion. One must conclude, then, that while many Judeans did reject Jesus as Messiah, their rejection was not based on a misunderstanding regarding whether or not the Messiah would be political. The literature of the period reveals that Judean messianic expectation varied widely and was not uniformly held by all Judeans. One theme that maintains throughout the literature, however, is that the Messiah will liberate the people from Roman rule.

The narrative of the Gospel of John reflects the historical reality that most Judeans rejected Jesus as the Messiah. In the story, the Judeans who reject Jesus as Messiah do so, not because he offers no way to liberation, but because his method of liberation is different

"heavenly figure" who is the "patron" of Israel. The text, however seems to identify the four beasts as the four actual empires, not their heavenly patrons, which leads the reader to identify "one like the son of man" in the same way, as Israel, not Israel's patron. Furthermore, 7:27 states that "kingship and dominion" are given to "the people" not to a heavenly patron, as one would expect if "one like the son of man" represents Israel's heavenly patron rather than Israel itself.

8. The idea of Jesus as the embodiment of Israel is found elsewhere in John. For example, Jesus speaks of himself as the temple (2:19–21), the center of the life of the nation, and as the "vine" (15:1–11), a symbol for Israel in the Hebrew Scriptures.

than that which they expect or want. He conquers through his martyrdom and prophetic word. In other words, Jesus proclaims and engages in nonviolent, prophetic resistance, calling people to begin living out the reign of God in the present. Many in his audience cannot comprehend him, nor can they follow him. The message that the text conveys through the rejection of Jesus as Messiah by the Judeans is that nonviolent prophetic resistance requires deep spiritual discipline and understanding that most people do not have. The story holds out hope that people can acquire this discipline and understanding if they join, through baptism and rebirth, the Jesus movement.

AN EGALITARIAN COMMUNITY

Jesus, in John, counters imperial/worldly rule by abolishing the hierarchies of that society and establishing an egalitarian ethic in the community that he founds. Probably the most powerful image in the gospel that conveys this idea is that of Jesus washing his disciple's feet (13:1–20). In this act he actually reverses the hierarchy, and we can hear in the background the anti-hierarchical teaching of the early church, reflected in the synoptic teaching, "Anyone who wants to become great among you must be your servant, and whoever wants to be first must be everyone's slave" (Mark 10:43–44, see also Matt 20:26–27, 23:11, Mark 9:37, Luke 22:26). In the passage in John, he not only teaches by example, but actually instructs them to wash each other's feet (13:14). The entire story, in fact, centers around this idea: the leader of the community, the anointed one, the king, lays down his life for others and instructs others to do the same, not for him, but for each other (15:12–17).

Another instance in which the egalitarian ethos emerges is in one of Jesus final statements to his disciples, the statement that he makes as he imparts the Holy Spirit to them: "If you forgive the sins of any they are forgiven, if you retain the sins of any, they are retained" (20:23, NRSV). With this pronouncement, he gives the entire community, all the people of the community, the power that in Judean law is reserved for priests. This authority is not merely religious authority; it is legal authority. In Judean law, the forgiveness of sins allowed people to participate socially and economically in the society. (It may have had similar significance throughout the first century Mediterranean world as evidenced by Caesar being proclaimed as the one who "wipes away our sins"). Jesus democratizes this authority, removing it from the purview of a privileged class. Forgiveness and reconciliation is now the responsibility and right of the whole community.

While this pronouncement is one isolated verse in John, the prevalence of this idea in the early church is reflected in the wider NT teaching of the priesthood of the whole community (Matt 18:15–20, Luke 17:3, Heb 10:19, 1 Pet 2:9, Rev 1:6, 5:9–10).

KINGDOM OF GOD

The term *kingdom of God* appears in the Fourth Gospel five times, twice in chapter 3 and three times in chapter 18, in Jesus' discussions with Nicodemus and with Pilate respectively. This term would have been understood by the original readers of the Fourth Gospel as a thoroughly political term, given the lack of distinction between the religious and political realms in their world, which resulted in the use of religious language by governments to substantiate their rule. For example the Roman emperor was believed to be divine, so the Roman Empire was also understood by its supporters to be a divine "kingdom" (the term for "kingdom," *basileia*, was used of the Roman Empire and so can be translated "empire" as well as "kingdom"). The "kingdom of God" would have been understood as a competitor with the divine kingdom of Rome.

Not only did the prevailing political/religious reality and practice result in an understanding of the term "kingdom of God" as a political and religious term, but so did the evolution of the term in the Hebrew Scriptures. The Hebrew Scriptures sometimes, usually in the Psalms, speak of God's kingdom as the whole earth (e.g., Ps 22:28; 103:19), but usually God's (or YHWY's) kingdom refers to Israel (e.g., 1 Chr 28:5; 2 Chr 13:8; Obad 21). In the post-exilic apocalyptic literature, we read of the revival of Israel which conquers the great empires (or "kingdoms") of the world to become the reigning kingdom established by God, a narrative that comes forth most clearly in Daniel. Daniel 2 tells of Nebuchadnezzar's dream, interpreted by Daniel, in which God establishes Israel as "a kingdom that shall never be destroyed" (2:44). Daniel 7 tells of Daniel's vision in which the "saints of the Most High," i.e., Israel, "receive the kingdom and possess the kingdom forever and ever" (7:18). This narrative of Israelite revival and sovereignty over the whole world may very well be the origin of the idea in John of the rebirth of Israel into the transnational kingdom of God that conquers the world.

When early Christians began talking about the kingdom of God, the authorities, especially the Judean authorities, understood this language as insurrectionary language,[9] an attempt to set up an autonomous political entity in territory claimed by the empire, and they were correct, even if they misunderstood much about the nature of this new kingdom. When NT writers articulated differences between the kingdom of God and the kingdom(s) of this world, they did not mean that the first is personal and interior and the second political, as is so often assumed today. The NT writers, through their texts, described a kingdom

---

9. The Judean authorities, composed of Judean elites who collaborated with Rome, understood clearly that Jesus' movement posed a threat to them and to Rome. The Roman authorities were slower to realize the threat because they were not as familiar with the Israelite traditions out of which this movement arose and because they were even less able to understand the alternative nature of this kingdom. While the Judean elite may have had difficulty comprehending all that Jesus talked about, the Roman authorities tended to have no comprehension whatsoever; Jesus' movement made no sense at all to them. This reality is reflected in all four gospel accounts of the interrogation of Jesus by Pilate. Pilate seems to have no comprehension of who or what he is dealing with.

with a different sort of politics, a different sort of social structure and economics. This kingdom would not rely on geographical boundaries, in fact it would be secret and subversive (see the parables in Matt 13 and Mark 4).

The secret and subversive character of the kingdom of God is why, in Luke, Jesus says, "The Kingdom of God is not coming with things that can be observed . . . for, in fact, the Kingdom of God is within/among you" (Luke 17:20–21, NRSV). In this passage, Jesus speaks to the secret and subversive way that the kingdom of God sneaks up on the kingdom(s) of this world to overthrow it/them: It sneaks in through people's hearts, through the new relational arrangements that they form with each other. Such an approach by the kingdom of God would not have been expected by most of Jesus' audience, people who wanted, or expected, it to come either through dramatic miraculous acts of God or through military conquest.

This same difference between the kingdom of God and the kingdom(s) of this world lies behind the famous statement in the Fourth Gospel that modern readers often interpret as a statement of the apolitical nature of the kingdom of God: Jesus responds to Pilate's query as to whether he is the "King of the Judeans" by saying, "My kingdom is not of/from this world. If my kingdom were of/from this world, my armed guard[10] would have fought to keep me from being handed over to the Judeans" (John 18:33–36). In this passage, Jesus stresses the heavenly nature of the kingdom of God, pointing out that it does not originate from the world's political milieu, so it is not of/from this world; Jesus' kingdom is not worldly. Being nonviolent and egalitarian, it does not participate in the violence and domination of the world's kingdoms or else Jesus'

10. I have translated the word *hupēretai* here as "armed guard" rather than "followers" (NRSV) or "servants" (NIV, KJV, ASV, NASB) because elsewhere throughout John, this word is used only for the police of the temple establishment. For John, this word seems to indicate an armed force. Outside of John, in the rest of the New Testament, this word is used more than half of the time to mean the police of the temple establishment.

armed guard would fight for him. As it is, he does not even have an armed guard. Jesus distinguishes the kingdom of God from the political entity of the Judeans that, he implies, does participate in the violence and domination of worldly politics and is, therefore, "of/from this world." (Interestingly, this passage does not use the term "Israel," which seems, in John, to be reserved for speaking of that entity which is being reborn into the kingdom of God, as opposed to the rule of the Judeans which has been co-opted by the kingdom(s) of this world, specifically the Roman Empire.) The difference between the kingdom of God and the kingdoms of this world results in Pilate misunderstanding the nature of the kingdom of God (just as Nicodemus before him had not been able to understand) and not taking it seriously; he cannot take seriously Jesus as a king with a kingdom.

AGAINST DEATH

For many readers and commentators of John, this gospel emphasizes the positive, beyond-death themes of resurrection and eternal life. Warren Carter, in his 2008 book, *John and Empire*, has shown how these themes of resurrection and eternal life, as well as the theme of ascension, literarily repel the political forces of death, the forces of empire and injustice. The following summarizes some of Carter's brilliant analysis of these ideas in John.

Eternal Life

While the Gospel of John uses the term "kingdom of God" five times, anyone familiar with the synoptic gospels might wonder why John's text does not use it much more frequently since this idea is so central to the narratives of Matthew, Mark, and Luke. Does this idea simply not play a major role in the Fourth Gospel? The answer to that question seems to be that instead of "kingdom of God," the Gospel of John prefers the term "eternal life" or simply "life," which carries an idea that is extremely similar to the idea of the kingdom of God.

The preference for the term "eternal life" or simply "life" may have arisen from the context of the book's final form in Asia Minor where Roman propaganda and imperial religion were prominent. The imperial propaganda declared Rome's "golden age" and that this "golden age" was "eternal."[11] The word translated into our English Bibles as "eternal" or "everlasting," *aiōnion*, is the adjectival form of the word for "age" or "era" and could be translated "agely" or "of the age" or "of the era."[12] The Fourth Gospel counters Rome's eternal golden age with "eternal (of the age) life."

The Roman propaganda proclaimed the empire's golden age to be a time of peace and prosperity. Virgil prophecies that the "age" will bring peace and that "The earth untilled will pour forth its first pretty gifts . . . Unbidden, the goats will bring home their udders swollen with milk . . . Every land will bear all fruits" (Virgil, *Ecl.*, 4.12–45)[13] Horace sings, "Bountiful crops and cattle, may Mother Earth deck Ceres [goddess of agriculture, corn and harvest] with a crown of corn; and may Jove's wholesome rains and breezes give increase to the harvest" (*Carmen Saeculare* 29–32).[14] These pronouncements sound much like those of the Hebrew prophets concerning the coming age of Israel's salvation:

11. Warren Carter, in *John and Empire*, cites a whole array of Roman sources that use this language for the empire. For example, Virgil, in *The Aeneid*, speaking through Anchises, the father of Aeneas, prophecies of Augustus Ceasar, "Here is Ceasar, and all the seed of Iulus destined to pass under heaven's spacious sphere. And this in truth is whom you so often hear promised to you, Augustus Ceasar, son of a god, who shall again establish a golden age" (*Aen.* 6.788). In the same work, Virgil has Jupiter declare about Rome, "I set no bounds in time or space; but have given empire without end whereby Romans will be lords of the world, and the nation of the toga" (*Aen.* 1.278). Livy describes Rome as a city founded to last "for eternity" (*Ab Urbe Condita*, 4.4.4; 28.28.11). Tibullus names it the "eternal city" (*The Elegies of Tibullus*, 2.5.23).

12. Carter, *John and Empire*, 208.

13. Cited in Carter, *John and Empire*, 223.

14. Ibid.

> The wilderness and the dry land shall be glad;
> the desert shall rejoice and blossom.
> Like the crocus it shall blossom abundantly . . . (Isa 35:1, NRSV)
> In that day, the mountains shall drip sweet wine,
> the hills shall flow with milk,
> and all the stream beds of Judah shall flow with water . . . (Joel 3:18,
> NRSV)
> The time is surely coming, says the LORD,
> when the one who plows shall overtake the one who reaps,
> and the treader of grapes the one who sows the seed;
> the mountains shall drip sweet wine
> and the hills shall flow with it. (Amos 9:13, NRSV)

Fulfilling the vision of the prophets and countering the propaganda of the empire, John's Jesus announces, "I have come that they might have life, and have it abundantly!"(10:10). And he performs miracles of abundance of food (6:1–14; 21:1–14) and of abundance of wine (2:1–11).

Jesus reverses the effects of the so-called "golden age" of the Roman Empire. This "golden age" was only golden for the elite who comprised 2–3 percent of the population. For the vast majority of people, life was often a daily struggle just to survive, a struggle marked by food shortages, malnutrition and the diseases and disabilities caused by malnutrition. Jesus' food and healing miracles reverse these tragedies and bring a true abundance of life, life that is "eternal" or "of the age."[15]

"Eternal" or "of the age" in John is an apocalyptic idea. Jewish and Christian apocalypticism spoke of the coming age of God's reign, when death and poverty and disease would be wiped out and there would be abundant life for all (e.g., Isa 25: 6–10; Rev 21: 3–4). Apocalypticism held that this coming age is even now breaking into the current world and making a space for itself (Luke 17:20–21). The Fourth Gospel's idea of "eternal life" speaks both to the future—"This is indeed the will of my father, that all who see the son and believe in him may have eternal life, and I will

---

15. Carter, *John and Empire*, 220–24.

raise them up on the last day," (6:40 NRSV, cf. 6:54)—and to the present—"the one believing in the son *has*[16] eternal life" (3:36). This idea is that of the eternal experienced in the present, i.e., the future age, the future reign, or "kingdom" of God, breaking into the present and making a space for itself in the kingdom(s) of this world through those who believe.

Resurrection

The ultimate way that Jesus reverses the effects of the empire is through resurrection. Not only does Jesus raise himself from the dead (10:17–18), he also extends resurrection to the whole community that he founds (3:15–16, 36; 6:40, 54), even giving them a foreshadowing of this reversal in the raising of Lazarus.

The way that resurrection reverses the effects of the empire lies not merely in that it reverses the murder perpetrated by the empire, i.e., reverses Jesus' crucifixion, but also that resurrection ultimately facilitates the final triumph of the kingdom of God. Resurrection does not merely constitute a saving reality for the individual, it recreates the whole world. The individuals of the community experience resurrection when the kingdom of God has finally arrived in all of its fullness, when the current kingdom(s) of this world have been defeated and judged and God's eternal reign of abundant life for all is finally established.

The concept of resurrection arises in the Hebrew Scriptures, canonical and noncanonical, in the context of resistance to empire.[17] Probably the earliest reference to resurrection is found in Daniel 12:1–3 that speaks of resurrection in terms of the final triumph of Israel over the Seleucid Empire. Later, 2 Maccabees 7 tells the story of the Seleucid king's execution by torture of seven brothers who refuse to eat pork. These brothers boldly proclaim their hope in resurrection as their final triumph over the empire.

16. *Echei,* present, active, indicative.
17. Carter, *John and Empire,* 216–8.

The Psalms of Solomon and 1 Enoch speak of resurrection in the context of the triumph of God's people over the Roman Empire.[18]

Ascension

Like the titles and roles for Jesus mentioned above, the final action by Jesus in the Gospel story should also be understood in the context of Roman imperial mythology, as a challenge to that mythology. Although the Gospel of John does not actually narrate the ascension, as do Mark and Luke-Acts, it does emphasize it as a major theme. Not only does Jesus use the verb "ascend" four times to describe his return to the father (3:13, 6:62, and twice in 20:17), he also constantly talks about his "coming" from God and "going" back to God (a topic that will be described fully in chapter 3).

Ascension in Roman imperial mythology was the privilege of the greatest of the emperors. The rhetoric of John's gospel seems to directly challenge this mythology: "No one has ascended into

18. *Pss. Sol.* 2:35 (31), 3:16 (12) and 5:15 (13) speak of resurrection; chapters 2 and 17 speak of the defeat of the Roman imperial invader. Carter summarizes these themes in 1 Enoch: ". . . resurrection is part of transformation of life on earth that involves judgment accomplished by the Son of Man and a significant change in sociopolitical structures. The main problem with the present age comes from the ruling elite, the 'kings,' 'mighty ones,' and 'the strong' who are sinners (46:4–5). They do not acknowledge or obey the source of their rule, the 'Lord of the Spirits,' the text's leading name for God (46:5b). Their ways on earth are marked by oppression, power, and wealth (46:7, 62:11). Judgment is effected on these oppressive 'wicked kings of the earth and the mighty landowners,' on 'the kings, the governors, the high officials, and the landlords' (62:3, 9), who have apparently denied access to the land and its produce as resources to sustain life (48:8). There is no mercy or resurrection for them (46:6), only annihilation (38:6), worms (46:6), and flames of judgment (54:6; 63:10). On the other hand, the righteous will experience a bodily resurrection (51:1–5) to a joyful and transformed life on earth (45:5; 61:5; 62:15–16; cf. 38:4; 48:7), 'without the oppression of sinners' (53:7) and without 'the sinners and the oppressors' (62:13). This transformed 'eternal life' (37:4; 48:7) depends on repentance (40:9), is never ending (58:3), and is lived in the 'garden of life' (61:12), reminiscent of the Garden of Eden. The end is a return to the beginning. Justice and life are the hallmarks of this resurrected somatic existence" (*John and Empire*, 217–8).

heaven except the one who descended from heaven" (3:13). And, just as with the "Son of God" polemic, John's rhetoric both debunks the divine status of the emperors by denying them ascension, saying that only Jesus has ascended to heaven and, at the same time, democratizes ascension by making it available, potentially, to all people when he speaks, not only of going back to the Father, but of coming back to take others with him (14:3).

A further way that Jesus subverts Roman imperial ascension is by the route that he takes back to God: He goes by way of the cross. Three times Jesus speaks of being "lifted up," by which he means both crucifixion and exaltation as king/Messiah/Son of God, with a strong allusion to ascension; in fact, the first "lifted up" saying occurs right after a statement about ascension (3:13–14). Also, when he speaks to his opponents and disciples saying that they cannot follow him where he is "going," he is cryptically speaking of going back to God by way of the cross (8:21–30, 13:31–38). In other words, the very method by which the empire tries to destroy him, he transforms into the method by which he ascends back to the Father, and by doing so, subverts imperial ascension.

FEAR OF ROME VERSUS FEAR OF GOD

John's Passion Narrative contains, perhaps, the most overt anti-imperial elements of any of the four gospels. Only in John's arrest scene do Roman soldiers, along with temple police, come to arrest Jesus (18:1–6). In Matthew and Mark, the arresting party appears to be a Judean mob (Matt 26:47, Mark. 14:43). Luke's version seems to start out the same as Matthew and Mark (22:47), but then adds temple police to the mix (22:52). Also, only in John does Pilate become afraid when he hears that Jesus claims to be the "Son of God," a title that would hit home with a Roman governor (19:8).

Probably the most striking aspect of John's Passion Narrative that brings out its anti-imperial message, however, is the portrayal of the Sanhedrin as fearing Rome more than

God. Frightened by the resurrection mania infecting the masses (11:45, 48; 12:12–19), they convene a special session in which they express their fear of Rome and resolve once and for all to have Jesus executed (12:45–53). Later, when they petition Pilate to have Jesus executed, the chief priests exclaim, "We have no king but Caesar!" (19:15), a declaration that would surely have been heard by others as a complete betrayal of their fellow Israelites who longed for liberation from the brutal Roman occupation and believed that the only true king of Israel is God. Some of the people held out hope for an earthly representative of God to reclaim the Davidic throne, but to proclaim a foreign king to be the "only king" would have been unthinkable for a pious Israelite, and the chief priests, at least publicly, were supposed to be the most pious of Israelites. Their public image was supposed to be as leaders of the people who negotiated with the Romans on behalf of their people. Although many of the common people knew that the chief priests and the Judean elite benefited from the occupation and were, in reality, traitors, this reality was not something that the chief priests wanted to admit publicly.

In no way should the actions of the high priests be understood as motivated only by fear in the sense that they are really trying to save the people from Rome's wrath. Their fear of Rome is rooted in their alliance with Rome. The high priesthood in the time of Jesus served at the pleasure of its Roman overlords. During the reign of Augustus Caesar, Herod the Great, having been proclaimed "King of the Judeans" by a Roman senate, returned to Israel and conquered it with Roman troops. Eventually, Herod replaced all the priests at the temple with his own handpicked priests who would be sure to do the bidding of Rome, including collecting tribute for Rome.[19] As time went on, Rome apparently became even more hands-on with respect to the high priesthood in Jerusalem. Josephus writes:

19. Horsley, *Liberation*, 40–41, 50–51.

Cyrenius, a Roman senator . . . being sent by Caesar to be a judge of that nation [Syria] . . . came into Judea, which was now added to the province of Syria . . .

[H]e deprived Joazar of the high priesthood, which dignity had been conferred on him by the multitude, and he appointed Annus [Annas], the son of Seth, to be high priest . . .

Tiberius Nero [many years later] deprived Ananus of the high priesthood, and appointed Ismael . . . He also deprived him in a little time, and ordained Eleazar, the son of Ananus, . . . which office, when he had held for a year, Gratus deprived him of it, and give the high priesthood to Simon . . . and when he had possessed that dignity no longer than a year, Joseph Caiaphas was made his successor. When Gratus had done those things, he went back to Rome, after he had tarried in Judea eleven years, when Pontius Pilate came as his successor.[20]

CONCLUSION

An understanding of the language and concepts of the Fourth Gospel in their literary, cultural and sociopolitical contexts lays the groundwork for a whole new understanding of the text for those of us who have grown up with individual piety as the only lens with which to comprehend the story that John tells. This new understanding, by placing the text in its original context, provides us with a reading that makes the text more coherent and also more relevant to the world that we live in.

20. *Ant.* 18.1, 26, 33–35, as quoted in Howard-Brook, *Becoming Children*, 382.

3

From God's Point of View

CONCERNING ORIGIN AND DESTINATION

> The wind blows where it wills, and you hear the sound of it,
> but you don't know where it comes from or where it goes, so it
> is with those born of the Spirit (John 3:8).

WHAT IS JESUS TALKING ABOUT WITH THIS CRYPTIC STATE-
ment? Are his followers to be people who blow around
like the wind, appear and disappear, now you see them, now you
don't? Are they mysterious people, quickly moving about so that
you can't keep up with them? Jesus makes this statement when trying to explain the concept of spiritual rebirth to Nicodemus, but
how does this cryptic statement help Nicodemus understand the
concept of being "born again"?

Jesus' words confuse and mystify Nicodemus. Nicodemus
cannot understand "heavenly things" (3:12). In the subsequent
chapters, Jesus continues to mystify and be misunderstood by people. Then in 8:14 he says something to the Jerusalem crowd that
sounds strangely similar to what he said to Nicodemus in chapter
3. He says to the Jerusalemites, "You don't know where I have come
from or where I am going." (The crowd has been discussing which

town Jesus is from and has been mystified by where he says that he is going.) Having noticed the similarities in the statements from 3:8 and 8:14, the reader may then notice that the issue of where Jesus *and* those born of the Spirit are from and where they are going constitutes a significant theme in the Gospel of John. (In addition to 8:14, see also 3:13, 31; 5:36; 6:58, 62; 7:27–29, 32–36, 41–42, 52; 8:42; 11:27; 12:26; 13:31–36; 14:3–6; 15:19; 16:5–10, 17, 28; 17:8, 11, 13, 22, 25; and 20:17.)

Although the origin and destination of Jesus and of those born of the Spirit is a mystery to Nicodemus and the crowd, these things are *not* meant to be a mystery to the reader of the text. The origin of Jesus should be exceedingly clear, if also paradoxical, to the reader. Jesus is from Nazareth (1:45), but he is also from God (1:1; 3:13, 31; 5:36; 5:58, 62; 16:28). Where Jesus is going becomes increasingly clear to the reader as the story unfolds: Jesus is going to the cross (3:14; 8:28; 12:32–33) after which he will rise (2:19; 16:16–22) and go back to God (16:28; 17:8–25; 20:17).

When Jesus departs from the earth, he leaves behind the Spirit who will make possible the rebirth of Jesus' followers (3:6–8; 14:16; 20:22). They are "born again" or "born from above" (3:3, 7) or "born of the Spirit" (3:5–9) or "born of God" (1:13). Having been reborn, the followers of Jesus, then, have the same paradoxical origin as Jesus: they were born in particular earthly locations, but from a "heavenly" perspective, they are from God, "born of God." Being followers of Jesus in the Spirit, they also have the same destination as Jesus: they follow in the way of the cross to resurrection and then to God (3:16; 5:28–29; 6:40; 11:25; 12:25–26; 13:36; 14:2–3). Such is their origin and destination that the world cannot understand.

This "heavenly" mystery, revealed to the reader, has enormous earthly consequences. Those who are born of God constitute a new family, a new community, even a new nation. They are "children of God . . . born not of blood or of the will of flesh or of the will of man, but of God" (1:12–13, NRSV).

More will be said about this new community later, but since it comprises much of the "heavenly" mystery that the text reveals to the reader, it is worth taking space right here to unpack the verse from the prologue quoted above. The three ways that the children of God are *not* born mark them off sociopolitically from the rest of society as a transnational community of peace, truth, light, love and justice.

First of all, they are born "not of blood." Raymond Brown points out that the word here for "blood" in the Greek is the plural form ("bloods") which is the Hebrew idiom for violence (see Mic 3:10, Hab 2:12, Hos 4:2, 1 King 2:5, 33, 2 King 9:7, 26). The children of God, therefore, are *not* children of violence, a major distinction in a world filled with violence, a world where boundaries between nations and tribes are often marked by violence. In the gospel narrative, this distinction marks off the followers of Jesus from the rest of the society whose father, according to Jesus, "was a murderer from the beginning" (8:44).

The climactic event of the story of this gospel, the crucifixion, demonstrates the nonviolent practice of the community. Jesus not only refuses to use violence against his enemies (in fact he stops Peter from using violence on his behalf and later explains to Pilate that the community that he has founded does not use violence as evidenced by the fact that his armed guard does not fight for him), but Jesus actually overcomes the forces of empire and domination through his prophetic martyrdom; the cross is his moment of victory. Three times he describes his crucifixion as his exaltation (3:14, 8:28, 12:34), the third time adding that it is the means by which he will "drive out" the "ruler of this world" (12:33), i.e., the forces of darkness that inhabit the worldly institutions of power. (This victory will be described in greater detail in chapter 7.) Jesus and the community that he founds use nonviolent prophetic witness and martyrdom to overcome their enemies and establish the kingdom of God. This new kingdom is a kingdom that wages a nonviolent warfare; it is a kingdom of peace.

Secondly, the children of God are born "not of the will of the flesh." The Gospel of John communicates its message through dualisms: earth/heaven, below/above, darkness/light, of this world/ not of this world, and flesh/Spirit. "The flesh" is "worldly," "of the earth," and "from below." "Flesh" is not evil, per se, but it is a lower aspect of human nature, one that is unable to understand "heavenly things" and it needs to be enlightened by the Spirit. Jesus came in the flesh so that people born of the flesh might be born of the Spirit.

To be "born of the flesh" means two things: 1) Location in a biological family/tribe/nation, the family "of the flesh." When someone is "born of the Spirit," that person is no longer limited by the biological family/tribe/nation but now is part of a spiritual family/tribe/nation. He or she becomes a "child of God." (More will be said of this below.) 2) Acting or understanding according to the flesh (see 3:6–12 and 8:15). The way or "will" of the flesh is the way of the world, a world that lives in darkness and cannot see the truth (3:19–21). The way of the world is the way of violence and tribalism and domination and, as we shall see right away, patriarchy.[1] In contrast, the community that Jesus founds is called to live by a higher "heavenly" way. It is called to live in the light (1:4–9; 3:21; 8:12; 11:9–10; 12:35–36, 46), in the Spirit of Truth (3:21; 4:23–24; 8:31–33, 40, 44–46; 14:6, 17, 15:26; 16:13; 17:17, 19; 18:37–38) and by the law of love (13:34–35; 15:9–13, 17). It is a community of light, truth, and love.

Thirdly, the children of God are born "not of the will of man." The term here for "man" is necessarily male, not the word that is usually used to refer to "people" or "humankind" (it cannot be made inclusive in the NRSV). Here the author makes the point that the children of God are not to be part of the patriarchal family system. The first-century Mediterranean world was highly patriarchal, and people found their identity and their primary community in the

---

1. Walter Wink suggests in *Engaging the Powers*, 61–63, that "flesh" (*sarx*) in the NT carries primarily a sociopolitical meaning.

family. Society in the Roman Empire was structured through interconnecting pyramids of familial patriarchies with the emperor conceived of as the grand patriarch at the top. The children of God are to form a family, a community, a nation, set apart from this system. To be born "not of the will of man," then, has considerable overlap with being born "not of the will of the flesh," but the former has specific implications for the ordering of the community. This new community is to be egalitarian. The egalitarian nature of this community is most powerfully demonstrated in 13:1–15 where Jesus washes his disciple's feet and instructs his disciples to wash each other's feet. Jesus' teachings about mutual love, service, and sacrifice (13:34–35; 15:9–13, 17) further explicate the egalitarian ethos of the community. The community that Jesus founds is an egalitarian community, a community of justice.

This new transnational family of God, its children born not of violence, nor limited by tribal identity or behavior, nor enslaved in the patriarchal system of the empire, demonstrates its ethos, in the story of John's gospel, through Jesus' speech and actions. One passage that communicates this ethos most clearly is 4:1–42 in which Jesus meets a Samaritan woman at a well. In this passage, Jesus crosses a major ethnic/national boundary to extend his community—here is the one place in the story of John where this new community becomes explicitly transnational. In addition to crossing an ethnic/national boundary, he also demonstrates a nonviolent embrace of the enemy (Judeans and Samaritans had a hostile relationship) and gender egalitarianism (men and women did not normally speak so freely in that culture). He demonstrates that this new community is "born not of blood, or of the will the flesh, or of the will of man."

So this new community of people born of the Spirit, born from above, born of God, constitutes a new sociopolitically radical entity that mystifies others by its "heavenly" practices and values. They do not partake of the tribalism and violence and domination of the world, but rather they take up the way of the cross, resisting these worldly ways. They travel in the spirit toward a life of abundance and victory through the cross. The world cannot understand the way of the cross; the way of the cross is countercultural. The way of the children of God is incomprehensible to the world. The world cannot comprehend where they are from or where they are going.

THE HEAVENLY PERSPECTIVE

The world's inability to comprehend Jesus and his message plays a major role in the Gospel of John. The way of Jesus, and of the community that follows after and believes in him, mystifies mainstream society, especially those in power but also those under the sway of the power elite.

The Gospel of John presents a view of reality from "above," a "heavenly" perspective. From this perspective, this gospel reveals society to be patriarchal/tribal, oppressive, and violent. People who live in and are conditioned by the systems of patriarchy, oppression, and violence have great difficulty comprehending a way that runs counter to the prevailing systems. Jesus shines like a light in a dark world, exposing the evil, but people prefer darkness (3:19–20); they can't understand the light (1:15).

By healing on the Sabbath and witnessing to the truth, especially the truth of who he is, Jesus exposes society's violent impulse. His interaction with the Jerusalem crowd at the Festival of Tabernacles illustrates this dynamic: Jesus accuses the crowd of "seeking to kill" him (7:19), an assertion that they emphatically deny (7:20). Despite their denial, he attributes their murderous impulse to his healing on the Sabbath (7:21–23). The people then begin to say, "Is this not the man whom they are seeking to kill?" (7:25). By the end of chapter 8, they actually pick up stones to kill Jesus, but he slips away. Jesus has exposed their violent nature, something that they were not even aware of themselves. He shines his light in the darkness on their evil desires. Through this interaction, the reader gets a heavenly perspective.

This view from "above" not only exposes evil in the world, it also reveals the "heavenly" perspective on the fundamental nature of reality. From the heavenly perspective, the strong do not always conquer the weak; those who wield the greater power of violence do not always prevail. There is a force more powerful than violence. John's narrative not only exposes and condemns the murderous impulse of society, it puts forth the opposite of violence as the antidote, the countervailing force that will overcome it. This opposite of murder is Jesus' willingness to be martyred.

In the same interaction with the Jerusalem crowd at the Festival of Tabernacles in which Jesus exposes their murderous intent, he simultaneously tells them about his crucifixion. He uses cryptic language, describing his execution on a cross ironically as something that he will do to elude their efforts to capture and kill him. When the temple police try to arrest him, he says, "I am with you a little while longer, and then I go to him who sent me. You will search for me but will not find me; and where I am, you cannot come" (7:33–34). This statement repels the advance of his enemies. The police are not able to apprehend him because Jesus stops them with his words. He cannot yet be arrested. It is not yet his hour. When he is finally arrested to be crucified, he will be going of his own volition somewhere they cannot follow even though they "search" for him. The police cannot capture Jesus or even follow him. They may have worldly strength and weapons, but Jesus possesses the power of God; his simple words deter their ability to arrest him.

The meaning and power of Jesus' words becomes clearer when he uses this same cryptic language again in chapter 8, still with the Jerusalem crowd. He says again, "I'm going away, and you will search for me, but you will die in your sin. Where I go, you cannot come." The Judeans seem to pick up on the fact that he is talking about his death, and they say, "He's not going to kill himself, is he? For he said, 'where I go you cannot come'?" Jesus then emphasizes that his perspective is from "above." He says that being from "above," he has much to "condemn." He then describes the crucifixion in terms of victory: "When you lift up the Son of Man, then you will know that I am [he]" (8:28). He speaks of the crucifixion as something that he will submit to of his own accord, in his own time, to elude their attempts to capture and kill him, and it will be the hour of his victory. This instance is the second of three in this gospel where Jesus describes his crucifixion as victory, saying that he will be "lifted up." Such is the heavenly perspective on Jesus' crucifixion.[2] This victory, this righteous martyrdom, is a path back to God that his enemies cannot follow.[3]

The heavenly perspective permeates the entire text of the Gospel of John, painting a portrait of Jesus as somewhat superhuman. It has been said that in this gospel, Jesus walks two feet above the ground. Although the historical Jesus may have exhibited many human frailties, the author of John stresses his divine aspect, the heavenly perspective that transcends the earthly perspective of his more human qualities. So just as the crucifixion is transformed from a shameful torturous death into an unqualified victory, so also the Galilean peasant sage of the synoptic tradition, so hesitant to reveal his true identity, is transformed into a more divine Son of

2. This perspective on the crucifixion is not wholly absent in the synoptic tradition. There, as well, Jesus describes the crucifixion as his hour of glory (e.g., compare Matt 24:29–30; 26:65 with the crucifixion narrative in Matt 27:45–54). But the synoptic gospels address it with a different tone. In those texts the reader feels the tragic weight of the crucifixion, and the heavenly perspective labors to break through, and when it finally does, it thunders forth in an earthquake (Matt 27:51), darkness over the entire land (Matt 27:45, Mark 15:33, Luke 23:44), and the rending of the temple curtain (Matt 27:51, Mark 15:38, Luke 23:45), dramatic elements which are absent in the Gospel of John. In John's gospel, the crucifixion is spoken of from the outset as victorious, the hour of Christ's victory. It is only as one gets closer to the passion event that one begins to feel the weight of this terrible murder.

3. Later in 14:31–38 Jesus again uses this same cryptic language to tell his disciples that he is going to the cross and that they cannot follow "now" but will follow "afterward."

God who gives philosophical discourses and boldly proclaims his identity. In John, Jesus remains in full control of the situation. He does not feel "the hour" coming upon him, as in the synoptic gospels. He does not pray that the cup of suffering be removed from him. In John's Gospel, no one takes Jesus' life from him. He lays it down of his own accord. He has the power to lay it down and the power to pick it back up again (10:18). When the authorities try to arrest him at the festival of booths, they are unable to. When the crowd tries to stone him, he slips away (8:58–59). Even when he is finally arrested in Gethsemane, the scene plays out to demonstrate that he is still in control: when he steps forward and declares "I am [he]," the soldiers and police fall to the ground (18:6). The message of John is that this poor Galilean peasant, with no army, not even citizenship in the empire, who uses no violence, who is crucified— he is the powerful one, he is the one in control, according to the heavenly perspective.

THE WISDOM OF GOD

The heavenly perspective that emphasizes the divinity of Jesus does so literarily by portraying him as the Wisdom of God. The Wisdom of God appears throughout the Bible as a person. The Hebrew Scriptures often personify God's wisdom as a woman. The New Testament proclaims that Jesus is the Wisdom of God (1 Cor 1:24, 30). The gospels of Matthew and Luke (and maybe also Mark) sometimes portray Jesus as the Wisdom of God by having Jesus say the sorts of things that Lady Wisdom of the Hebrew Scriptures might say, such as when he issues the invitation "Come to me . . . and I will give you rest; take my yoke upon you and learn from me . . ." (Matt 11:28–30; compare to Sir 6:24–31; 24:19 and 51:23–27) or declares, referring to himself, "Wisdom is justified by all her children" (Luke 7:35, very similar to Matt 11:19). Yet although the synoptic texts occasionally slip into personifying Jesus as Wisdom, the Gospel of John begins by portraying Jesus as the Wisdom of God and maintains this portrait relentlessly throughout the entire narrative.

John's gospel opens up by speaking of Jesus as the Word of God, and while the Hebrew tradition of the Word of God contains some of the literary background for these statements, the Wisdom of God tradition supplies just as much or more of the literary background. According to the Wisdom literature, Wisdom existed with God "in the beginning" and "before the beginning of the earth" (Prov 8:22–23, Wis 6:22, Sir 24:9) just as Jesus in John 1:1 (and 17:5). John's prologue proceeds to call Jesus the "light of all people" (1:4) and the "true light that enlightens all people" (1:9). In the same way, Wisdom is a "reflection" of God's light (Wis 7:26) and is better than natural light (Wis 7:10–29), and of course, Wisdom's function is to enlighten, to teach, people. The last section of the prologue of John, in 1:14, describes the incarnation of Christ, saying, "The word became flesh and tabernacled among us." Sirach speaks of Wisdom searching for a resting place among the peoples of the earth and finally making her "tabernacle" in Israel (24:8). Wisdom and Christ the "Word" both find their entry point among humankind by making their "tabernacle" in Israel. Baruch also speaks of a kind of incarnation of Wisdom: "She appeared on Earth and lived with humankind" (3:37, NRSV).

While the function of the word of God in the Hebrew Scriptures is often that of prophecy, it sometimes functions to instruct and teach (e.g., Isa 2:3, Ps 119) just like the wisdom of God. The two concepts can be very close, which explains why the author could use the idea of the Word of God with so much Wisdom imagery. But the Wisdom of God is the only one of the two that becomes personified in the Hebrew Scriptures and the only one that is said to descend to dwell among humankind. Also, while the Word is implicit at creation, "in the beginning," in that God creates the world by word, the Word is not explicitly said to have existed with God "in the beginning" as is the case with Wisdom.

The prologue of John begins the characterization of Jesus as Wisdom through its description of him as the Word of God. As the narrative of John proceeds, Jesus' Wisdom persona manifests through Jesus' behavior: Jesus acts and talks like Lady Wisdom. In the Hebrew Scriptures, Wisdom walks the streets crying out to the people (Prov 1:20–21; 8:1–4; 9:3) and gives long discourses in the first person. In John, Jesus often cries out in public places (7:28, 37; 13:44) and gives long discourses, often using "I am" statements. Wisdom exhibits no shyness about her own importance and what she has to offer people and sharply warns about what will happen if her message is rejected. Likewise in John, Jesus (in contrast to his speech in the other Gospels), speaks loudly about who he is, in a manner that seems rather extreme, the sort of statements that might lead modern hearers to conclude that he is psychotically delusional. When Jesus' extreme statements are challenged, he counters with harsh rebukes, such as charging his opponents with being children of the devil (8:44). Wisdom declares that she leads people to life and immortality. Jesus does the same. Wisdom invites people to eat her bread and drink her wine (Prov 9:5, Sir 24:19–21). Jesus issues the same invitation (John 6:22–59). Understanding the literary persona of Wisdom that is invoked in the narrative of John's gospel to portray Jesus, greatly aids the reader in comprehending Jesus' extraordinary behavior in this text.

Jesus' statements at the Feast of Tabernacles illustrate this feature of John's narrative. When speaking of his going away, saying, "You will search for me, but you will not find me; and where I am, you cannot come" (John 7:34, also 8:21, 14:33, 36), he again sounds like Lady Wisdom who says, "they will call upon me, but I will not answer, they will seek me diligently, but will not find me" (Prov 1:28–29, NRSV). Not all of Jesus' statements in John follow so closely the actual words of Wisdom in the Hebrew Scriptures, but his overall behavior and persona do consistently follow the pattern of Lady Wisdom throughout this gospel.

The Gospel of John presents Jesus as Wisdom, fully in control of his situation, powerful in word and deed. From a worldly point of view, he may have been a mere peasant with no wealth or power, but from God's point of view, he is the Light of Life, the Word that has overcome the world (16:33).

4

Israel Reborn

A S MENTIONED IN CHAPTER 3, THE NEW COMMUNITY OF THE
Spirit in John transcends nationalism, tribalism, and familial patriarchies. Those born of the Spirit may have been born in particular tribes and families, but from a heavenly perspective, they are from God, they have been reborn as God's children, part of God's family, part of God's kingdom. For people of the first-century Mediterranean world, the family, clan, and tribe were the primary source of identity. To break with that community and to join another was like being born all over again, one's total identity was transformed, reoriented. To be "born again," in John, means a radical reorientation into a new community, a new family, and a new nation.

This new nation, however, is not just some completely new entity that falls out of the sky, even though the text almost says that when it emphasizes over and over that Jesus descended from heaven to create a new community of those who are born of God. While emphasizing the heavenly nature and origin of the new community, the text also emphasizes that this new nation arises out of the old: it is a new Israel, Israel reborn. The text seems to say that it is Israel that descends from heaven in the person of Jesus.

The formation of this new community/nation plays a central role in the story world of the gospel, and it also seems to have been the reality out of which the gospel was written. Many scholars believe that the gospel of John was the product of a Christian community, probably in Asia Minor during the late first century, that was separating itself from the Judean community as a result of having been expelled from the synagogue. This gospel, consequently, tells the story of the formation of a new community that is being called out from among the Judeans. This new community, therefore, has its roots in the Israelite nation and also transcends that nation. This chapter will follow the narrative of the first three chapters of the Gospel of John as it reveals the rising of this new community that is Israel transformed.

A NARRATIVE OF (RE)BIRTH

The text of the gospel begins with a prologue that speaks of a new "children of God . . . born not of the will of man" (1:12), i.e., born outside the patriarchal family/clan/tribe system. The prologue sets the stage for a story about the birth of a new family/community/ nation. After this prologue, the story of the Gospel begins.

Israelite Beginnings

The story begins with a passage about John the Baptist (1:19–34) that roots the advent of Jesus and his community in Israelite prophecy. John the Baptist identifies himself as the voice of Isaiah, preparing the way for Jesus and the community that he founds. This image of an Israelite prophet in the "wilderness" baptizing the masses strongly suggests an Israelite renewal movement. By the time the text of this gospel was being written, baptism had come to be understood as the public ritual of entry into the new community/nation of the church, but the church still remembered that baptism was an Israelite practice, sometimes for the initiation of people into the Israelite nation. The "wilderness" is the place where Israel was born as a nation after the exodus from Egypt. An Israelite prophet in the "wilderness" performing the ritual of baptism would forcefully convey for the original readers of this text that the people are returning to the place of the nation's birth to be reinitiated as a nation. John's baptism ministry signals the rebirth of Israel.

The story then proceeds with the calling of the first disciples, the beginning of the new community (1:35–51). This section invokes images of the stories of Israel's beginnings. Jesus calls Nathaniel "a true Israelite in whom there is no deceit" and then proceeds to tell him "you will see heaven opened and the angels of God ascending and descending on the Son of Man" (1:47–51). These declarations invoke for the reader the stories of Jacob, one of Israel's patriarchs, the patriarch after whom the nation is named— Jacob's name was changed to "Israel" and the nation of Israel is often referred to in the Hebrew Scriptures as "the house of Jacob."

When Jesus calls one of these first disciples a "true Israelite," and that disciple in turn calls Jesus "the King of Israel," the narrative signals that the new community, this new nation that is being born, is firmly rooted in the historic nation of Israel. The historic Israelite nation provides the nourishment, the fertile ground out of which this new Israel can emerge. Israel is not to be discarded and forgotten. Its stories, its traditions, its laws, and its prophecies are precisely that which give rise to this new kingdom of God. Even the idea that a new "true" Israel will rise up out of the old has its origin in Israelite prophecy. The prophets speak of a "remnant" that will give rise to a new Israel after the old has been crushed. Isaiah speaks of Israel as a stump out of which a new shoot sprouts (Isa 40:3).

Jesus calls Nathaniel "a true Israelite in whom there is no deceit." This pronouncement references the tradition that "Jacob" meant "the deceiver" and that, in fact, Jacob did deceive both his father Isaac, to steal the birthright and paternal blessing from his brother Esau, and his father-in-law, Laban (Gen 25:19—30:43).

Some commentators have interpreted Jesus' pronouncement to signal the superiority of the new community/nation to the old Israel, i.e., Jacob was a deceiver, but the disciples of this new community are "true" and "without deceit." Another interpretation, however, is possible. When Jacob's name was changed to "Israel" after wrestling with an angel, he presumably was no longer a deceiver. The story goes on to tell of how he reconciled with Esau (Gen 32:22—33:17; earlier in the story, he had reconciled with Laban). So Jesus' pronouncement may merely signal the rebirth of the "true" Israel, the emerging of "the remnant."

Jesus goes on to say, "You will see Heaven opened and the angels of God ascending and descending on the Son of Man." The Hebrew of the original text in Genesis that is being referenced (28:12) can be translated to mean that the angels went up and down a ladder or up and down on Jacob, and some rabbis argue for the second interpretation. Using this alternate reading, Jesus continues to underscore the rebirth of Israel. Just as through the patriarch who fathered the twelve tribes of Israel, God opened up a portal between heaven and earth, so God would again open up a portal through Jesus whose advent gives birth to a new Israel, beginning with the twelve disciples. The text of John makes much of this portal between heaven and earth. The gospel repeatedly speaks of Jesus having descended to earth from heaven to lead back all who follow after him.

Perhaps the place of the original story has significance as well. Jacob's vision occurred at Bethel, one of the early sites of the tabernacle that would later become the temple in Jerusalem. The tabernacle/temple was understood to be the locus of the portal between heaven and earth. The prologue has already identified Jesus with the tabernacle (1:14), and very shortly, in the gospel text, Jesus will make the point that he is the temple (2:13–22), i.e., the portal between heaven and earth. Written at a time after the destruction of the temple in Jerusalem, an event that caused incredible existential crisis for the Judeans, such an assertion would be powerful.

The Wedding at Cana

The text proceeds with the story of the wedding feast at Cana where Jesus turns water into wine. Marriage in the Hebrew Scriptures often served as a metaphor for the relationship between God and God's people.[1] Feasting, rich food, and an abundance of wine often symbolized the messianic days.[2] The New Testament writers combined these themes of marriage and feasting in the image of the wedding feast to symbolize Jesus coming as the Messiah to call forth his community of disciples (who are symbolized as the bridesmaids or guests at the wedding or the wife or bride).[3] In Matthew and Luke, Jesus uses the metaphor of the wedding feast in his teaching. In John the wedding feast is an event, narrated in the story, in which Jesus participates. Jesus' teaching in Matthew and Luke identifies Jesus as the bridegroom or implies through parable that Jesus is the bridegroom. In John, since the wedding feast is an event in the story and not just a teaching metaphor, the identification of Jesus as the bridegroom has to be indirect since Jesus never actually marries. Jesus appears as a guest at the wedding (along with his disciples), he changes the water into wine, and the chief steward attributes the new wine to the bridegroom. So Jesus is indirectly identified with the bridegroom (and his disciples remain the guests as in Matthew and Luke). Later in chapter 3, John the Baptist actually identifies Jesus as a "bridegroom" (3:29).

1. Isa 62:4–5; 54:5; Jer 2:2, 32; 3:1–10; Hos 1–3; Ezek 16:8–63.

2. Isa 25:6; 55:1–2; Amos 9:13–14; Enoch 10:19; 2 Bar 29:5.

3. Matt 9:15; 22:1–14; 25:1–12; Mark 2:19; Luke 5:34; 12:36; 14:8; Rev 19; 21:2, 9. Also Eph 5:22–32 and 2 Cor 11:2 use the marriage image for Christ and the church, so the community of disciples is the bride or wife, as in the Hebrew Scriptures.

This story of the wedding feast, on the heels of the calling of the first disciples, gives the reader the metaphor, through the narrative, of Jesus coming as the bridegroom to call forth his community. The images are fluid. The disciples, as in Matthew and Luke, are guests at the wedding feast, and Jesus is only indirectly identified with the groom. The mother of Jesus, in the first of her two guest appearances in this gospel, also plays a role in this imagery.

In this fluidity of images, Jesus' mother too symbolizes the community of disciples, for she is the church. She is also Israel and the first woman, Eve. Jesus addresses his mother as "woman," not the customary way for a man to address his mother, but not rude either, just strange. He addresses her this way both times that she appears in this gospel: at the Cana wedding and later at the cross. This odd form of address alerts the reader that there is some literary significance to it. The literary background can be found in the following: 1) Eve, in Genesis 2–3 is called "woman" (same word in the ancient Greek translation of the Hebrew Scriptures); 2) The author of Revelation (a text written about the same time as the Gospel of John) picks up on the "woman" of Genesis 2–3 for the image of the "woman" in Revelation 12, whom most commentators agree symbolizes Eve, Mary, the church, and possibly Israel (she seems to symbolize the people of God, which is the church and Israel out of whom the church arises); 3) The early church understood Mary to represent the New Eve and the church[4]; 4) The Hebrew Scriptures often use a woman to symbolize Israel 5) The New Testament uses the image of a woman for the church.

The Gospel of John links the two events in which Jesus' mother (not actually called "Mary" in this gospel) appears. At the Cana wedding, Jesus speaks of his "hour," a term which Jesus uses in this

---

4. Brown, *John I–XII*, 108, cites the following: Justin Martyr's *Dialogue with Trypho*, c 5; Patrologia Graeca-Latina, 6:712; and Irenaeus *Against Heresies*, 3.22:4; Patrologia Graeca-Latina, 7:959.

gospel to refer to the crucifixion.[5] The story of the wedding ends with Jesus' glory being revealed (2:11). In John, the hour of Jesus' glory is the cross (12:23). The wine symbolizes not only the abundance of the messianic time, but throughout the New Testament it also symbolizes the blood of Jesus.[6] At Cana we read of water and wine. At the cross, water and blood flow from Jesus' side (19:34).

At Cana the disciples come to believe in Jesus (2:11); they become children of God according to the earlier passage in 1:12 ("he gave . . . those who believed in his name the right to become children of God"), and mother church, the "woman," is there at their (re)birth. At the cross, Jesus says to his mother, "Woman, behold your son." To the archetypal disciple, "the disciple whom Jesus loved," he said "behold your mother" (19:26–27).

The Cana wedding foreshadows the crucifixion. In the Cana wedding, Jesus speaks of his "hour." His mother is present, the water and wine are present, and the disciples believe and are (re)born. At the cross, the "hour" has come, water and blood flow from Jesus' side, and the relationship between the woman and the archetypal disciple is solidified. She is the mother of the disciple community. She is Israel and the church.

Mary, an Israelite woman, carries the image of the New Israel—the church emerging out of the old Israel—giving (re) birth to the disciple community. In chapter 3 Jesus will speak of being born again. These early passages, however, provide only a foreshadowing; the actual rebirth of the disciples cannot take place until after the crucifixion, even after the resurrection, when Jesus breathes on them the Holy Spirit so that they are born of the Spirit (20:22). The Cana wedding only points to this event. Jesus' hour has not yet come.

5. 7:30, 8:20, 12:23, 12:27, 13:1, 16:32, 17:1
6. See 6:53–56

The Destruction and Resurrection of the Temple: Israel's Death and Rebirth

The next passage, 2:13–25, finds Jesus cleansing the temple and then speaking of its destruction, by which he really means, so the text claims, the destruction of his own body. Through this clever literary maneuver, the author alludes to the destruction of the temple in 70 CE and puts forth Jesus as its replacement. While the Jesus of the gospel story may be speaking of his own crucifixion and resurrection, the author wants very much to bring to mind the destruction of the actual temple. This cataclysmic event constitutes much of the historical context for the setting of the Christian community that produced the Gospel of John. The destruction of the temple in 70 CE involved more than just the end of Israel's religious geographical center. The destruction of the temple occurred as a consequence of the failed Judean uprising against Rome from 66–70 CE. Not only the temple, but the entire city of Jerusalem was destroyed, as well as many other Judean towns and villages. Thousands of Judeans were slaughtered, thousands were enslaved, and thousand fled into a new Diaspora. The destruction of the temple served as the focal representational event for the destruction of Israel. The great tree of Israel had been cut down and only a stump, "the remnant," remained, some in Judea and many more in the Diaspora, such as those in Asia Minor.

The destruction of Israel and its temple produced an existential crisis for the Judeans. Without their autonomous homeland and temple, that even the Diaspora Judeans could look to and sometimes travel to, who would they be? Where would they find their center as a people? How would God be with them?

Some Judeans turned to the study and veneration of Torah as their existential and spiritual center, giving rise to rabbinic Judaism. The followers of Jesus proclaimed Jesus and his church as the new Israel, i.e., Israel reborn.

This text, presenting Jesus' body as the replacement of the temple, provides the path of rebirth for Israel. Jesus embodies not only the temple, but Israel itself, so the death of Israel is transferred to Jesus' body, and Israel finds resurrection/rebirth in the resurrection of Jesus.[7]

Israel Reborn through the Cross

The next passage (3:1–21) continues the theme of the rebirth of Israel through Jesus' death and resurrection, specifically focusing on the cross as the way to rebirth.

Nicodemus, the Pharisee, represents the rabbinic Judean community at the time the gospel was written. Specifically he represents some of the leaders of that community who contemplated joining the Gospel community. Wes Howard-Brook suggests that there were many in the rabbinic community who wanted to explore membership in the Jesus community but were too afraid to express their desires openly, so they are represented in the text as a Pharisee coming to Jesus secretly, "by night" (3:2). Howard-Brook argues that Jesus' immediate response to Nicodemus' inquiry, the challenge to be born again/from above, reflects the call of the church to these secret seekers to join the church publicly. Joining this community publicly would involve a radical reorientation. Anyone joining the church publicly ran a high risk of being cut off from family, community, and synagogue—the church would be their new family. In other words, they would have to be born

7. Jesus as temple and as Israel has already been presented in the imagery of the text: The prologue uses wisdom imagery for Jesus, saying that he "*tabernacled* among us" (1:14). Later, in 2:51, Jesus calls himself "The Son of Man," a collective image from Daniel for the nation of Israel. Jesus states in this passage that angels will ascend and descend on him, imagery that invokes the Jacob story at Bethel, which later became the place of Israel's tabernacle. This Jacob story was likely a supporting story for the placement of the tabernacle at Bethel. Later in John, Jesus will call himself the "true vine." The image of a vine was one that was used in the Hebrew Scriptures for Israel (Jer 5:10–11; Hos 10:1; Jer 6:9; Ps 80:8; Isa 5:1–9).

all over again into a new family. This radical reorientation would put them in a position to understand things that they could not previously understand. Only by definitively joining this persecuted community that practiced a countercultural ethic, could they begin to understand the wisdom in this ethic or "way." In the words of this passage, they would be able to understand "heavenly things" (3:12) and "see the Kingdom of God" (3:3).

Nicodemus responds to the challenge to be born again by expressing incomprehension: "How can anyone be born having become old? He can't enter a second time into the mother's womb and be born, can he?" (3:4). The author uses this exaggerated statement of incomprehension to drive home the difference in perspective between those who have broken ties with their families and communities to join the church and those who have not (the concept of rebirth was already present in Judaism and used for converts to the faith due to the change in their sociopolitical status, so Nicodemus' statements of incomprehension are likely a literary device to serve the message). Jesus continues to baffle Nicodemus by speaking about the origin and destination of his followers (3:7–8). The origin of his followers, as stated earlier, is God, so they are born of God or "born from above." This passage will bear out that the destination of Jesus' followers is the cross (or heaven through the cross).

Nicodemus continues to express incomprehension, and Jesus' statements highlight Nicodemus' inability to comprehend "heavenly" matters (3:11–12). Jesus then speaks again of origin and destination, specifically his own, but by implication those of his followers as well. He speaks of being from God and going back to God (3:13). In the next verse he talks about the necessity of the cross as part of that destination: "so must the Son of Man be lifted up" (3:14). For one to be born again, to have the same origin and destiny as Jesus and his followers, one must go the way of the cross, a way that is incomprehensible to those who have not taken the bold leap of definitively joining the community.

Earlier, in verse 5, Jesus states that to see the kingdom of God, one must be "born of water and Spirit." Jesus refers here to the two baptisms that John the Baptist spoke of in 1:31–33, baptism into water and baptism into the Spirit. Water baptism, for the Johannine community at the time this gospel was written, constituted the public ritual of entry into the church that, by virtue of the social upheaval created by such a public act, would push one into the second baptism, the baptism in the Spirit. Spirit baptism was the journey with Jesus through life, death, and resurrection. Baptism in water was the ritual, baptism in the Spirit was the reality experienced in life. The water baptism ritual came to symbolize, in the early church, being baptized into Christ's death and raised with him in his resurrection.[8] Spirit baptism referred to the reality that water baptism pointed to. Spirit baptism was the reality of following Jesus, in this new community, through life, death, and resurrection. Both baptisms, therefore, were required to be born again/born from above. The process of being born again began with water baptism but was not complete until one had traveled in the Spirit with Jesus through death and resurrection. This experience is what it meant to be "born of the Spirit" or "born of God." (Later in 16:21, the text will again speak metaphorically about birth through death.)

To clarify: to be "born of water" in John, is to undergo the ritual of water baptism. To be "born of the Spirit" is the same as to be "born of God" or to be "born from above," which, as described above, refers to the experience of leaving one family to join another so that one is "born" into the new family, "born again." To be "born of the Spirit" is, therefore, the reality of radical reorientation into a persecuted, countercultural community that follows the way of the cross. "Baptism in the spirit" speaks to the experience of being plunged, as it were, into this radical reorientation, being birthed into the crucified community.

---

8. Rom 6:3–4.

In summary, this passage (3:1–23) expands on the theme of rebirth after a passage (2:13–25) that speaks of the destruction or death of Israel. In the first passage, the death of Israel is transferred to Jesus' body and finds resurrection. In the second passage, an Israelite leader is invited to be reborn through baptism, participation in the death and resurrection of Jesus.

Baptism as Purification

The next passage (3:22–30) continues the theme of baptism, specifically in water. As has been shown above, the previous passage links together baptism, rebirth, and crucifixion/resurrection. This passage links water baptism to the water at the Cana wedding through the use of the word "purification." The author uses "purification" to refer both to water baptism (3:25) and to the purpose of the water that would normally go into the jars at Cana (2:6). Further linkage between this passage and the passage of the Cana wedding occurs through the wedding imagery in this passage, imagery that identifies Jesus as the bridegroom, an identification that is made indirectly in the Cana wedding passage (as noted above).

The literary linkage between this passage and that of the Cana wedding, specifically linking the water for the baptism of John and Jesus to the water for Judean ritual purification, may shed light on John's statement, that he must decrease while Jesus must increase (3:30). John and his baptismal ministry and the water for Judean purification rites may represent the old Israel, which the author(s) wants to suggest is fading as the new Israel rises. The change is not a mere replacement, as many Christian interpreters have maintained, but rather a transformation. A purification rite rooted in the practices of the old Israel carries forward; Jesus and his disciples baptize, presumably, just as John baptized.

Writing in the gentile setting of Asia Minor in the late first century after the destruction of the temple, the community that produced John's gospel found itself in a context that highlighted the transnational nature of the Gospel message. The old ways of Israelite nationalism would lose relevance in such a setting. Acts records the struggle of the church, as it spread to the gentiles, to figure out how much of Torah, the primary national document of Israel, would be binding in the new context for gentiles (Acts 15:1–21). Perhaps the Gospel of John reflects this struggle at a much later stage, both emphasizing the old Israelite roots of the church but also presenting this new community as a new transnational Israel.

Concerning purification specifically, the Gospel of John seems to say that since Israel finds rebirth through the cross, this new community is a crucified community that finds its purification through the cross. In Cana the water turns to wine, which symbolizes blood; water and blood flow from Jesus side; baptism re-enacts the crucifixion and resurrection; and Jesus speaks of persecution as purification in 15:1–3. The new transnational Israel arises purified through the cross.

A NEW ISRAEL RISING
(A REVIEW WITH SOME NEW INFORMATION)

The first passage after the prologue concerns the baptismal ministry of John and also of Jesus. John is said to be baptizing in water (1:26), whereas Jesus will baptize with the Spirit (1:33). John appears and operates in the tradition of the Israelite prophets, even though the times of the prophets were said to have ended. John introduces Jesus as the one who will bring the Holy Spirit (1:32–33), signifying the messianic era.

After Jesus is introduced, the text proceeds with the calling of the first disciples, invoking imagery of Israel's beginnings. This imagery signals that Israel is being reborn. Israel has been subjected to occupation by the Romans, but Israel is being revived through Jesus in this messianic time. Jesus even refers to himself in this passage as "the Son of Man," an image from Daniel of Israel overcoming and breaking free of the empires that have ruled over it (see Daniel 7).

The next passage tells of a wedding feast, another image signaling the messianic days, the remarriage between God and God's people, leading to the rebirth of Israel. The text uses the images of water and blood, symbolizing water baptism and the crucifixion/resurrection that water baptism ritually reenacts. This story, as shown above, points forward to the crucifixion.

The gospel proceeds with a passage that alludes to the final destruction of the Israelite nation in 70 CE. In this passage, Israel through its temple in Jerusalem is transferred to Jesus' body and finds rebirth through his destruction and resurrection.

The next passage tells of a Judean leader coming to Jesus by night. Jesus tells him that he must be reborn of water and the Spirit (3:5), the baptisms of John and Jesus. The way of rebirth is the way of the cross (3:14).

Then the text turns to actual water baptism again. This time both John and Jesus baptize with water, but the point of the passage is that John's ministry must decrease as Jesus' ministry increases. The sun is setting on the old Israel. John is the last prophet. The new Israel emerges in the ministry of Jesus.

Through Jesus, Israel will not only survive the calamities that are about to come upon it in 70 CE at the hands of the Romans, Israel will defeat the imperial beast through the prophetic word, the Wisdom of God.

In the next passage, 3:31–36, John the Baptist (or the narrator) begins speaking of Jesus as the Son of God again, proclaiming that he is "above all" and that God has put "all things in his hands." The "Son" language here has two referents: In the Roman Empire, the "Son of God" was the emperor. In the Hebrew Scriptures, the "Son of God" is Israel (Hos 11:1). Jesus as Israel, the text declares, is more powerful than Caesar.

5

Jesus is Torah

THREE TIMES IN JOHN, WE READ THAT FOLLOWERS OF JESUS are being or will be expelled from the synagogue: 9:22; 12:42; and 16:2. These occurrences plus the structure and content of arguments that this gospel appears to want to advance have led many scholars to believe that Jesus' conflicts and debates with Judeans that are recorded in the text of John reflect the conflicts and debates of the Johannine community with the larger mainstream Judean synagogue community,[1] from which the Johannine community was being expelled, at the time that the text was written. While much of the conflict centers on Jesus' identification of himself as divine, bound up in that identification are the issues of the interpretation of Torah, the continuance of Israel as a nation, and resistance to Rome.

After the fall of Jerusalem and the virtual destruction of Israel, much, though not all, of the emerging rabbinic Judean community effectively put aside resisting the empire and turned their

1. The conflicts and debates in the text of John are also consistent with the conflicts that the historical Jesus likely had with the Judean authorities. He very likely clashed with them over their interpretation of the law and how to keep the Sabbath holy, and he was very likely perceived by the Judean ruling class as both a threat to their power and someone who might bring down on them the wrath of Rome.

energy inward toward intense study and veneration of the written Torah, buoyed by a precarious peace with Rome.[2] Many segments of the wider Judean community, however, did not fall in line with this position and practice. The Johannine community constituted one such dissident segment.

RESISTANCE VERSUS NONRESISTANCE

The quiet Torah study of the emerging rabbinic community developed from the very beginning as a strategy for survival. Yochanan ben Zakai , a prominent Pharisee living in Jerusalem during the Judean uprising against Rome in 66–70 CE, had himself smuggled out of Jerusalem in a coffin so that he could negotiate with the Roman general Vespasian. Upon meeting with Vespasian, ben Zakai correctly predicted that Vespasian would become the emperor of Rome and that the temple would soon be destroyed. Vespasian rewarded ben Zakai by allowing him to convene a rabbinical school in Yavneh after the war. The school in Yavneh became the center of rabbinic Judaism.

While mainstream rabbinic Judaism built itself on this precarious peace with Rome, many Judeans throughout the empire maintained an attitude of resistance and were eventually joined by some within the rabbinic community who found peace with Rome to be unsustainable. This posture of resistance manifested in two subsequent wars of rebellion with Rome: the Kittos War, 115 CE, and the Bar Kochba Revolt, 132 CE. Both wars featured amazing successes by the Judean rebels but ultimately ended in defeat for them.

The Johannine community, along with much of the rest of the early church, also maintained an attitude of resistance, but eschewed violence, opting instead for a nonviolent, prophetic resistance. This is not to say that these early Christians were unique among Judeans in choosing nonviolent prophetic resistance.

2. Cohen, *Maccabees to the Mishnah*, 216.

Nonviolent prophetic resistance to empire had already established somewhat of a venerable tradition among the oppressed Judeans. Judean apocalyptic literature of that period constituted in itself nonviolent prophetic resistance against the empire. For example, the book of Daniel portrays four Judean men engaging in civil disobedience in regard to the laws of the Babylonian empire, and then the book goes on to prophesy the fall of that empire as well as of successive empires that ruled over Israel.

Furthermore, the Judeans in Palestine during and shortly after the time of Jesus demonstrated nonviolent resistance against Roman attempts to humiliate them. In one case, after Pontius Pilate introduced Roman standards into Jerusalem which bore the image of Caesar, a large group of Judeans gathered in the city and lobbied Pilate for six days to have the standards removed. On the sixth day, Pilate surrounded the people with his soldiers and threatened to execute them if they did not disband. Rather than disband their peaceful protest, they challenged the Roman governor to kill them by showing him their bare necks. Pilate relented and had the standards removed from the city.[3] This tradition of Judean nonviolent resistance no doubt inspired Jesus and the communities that followed his teachings.

The posture of resistance among the Jesus-follower communities was, arguably, uneven. While they may have all practiced, or attempted to practice, a social and economic egalitarianism, as well as a nonviolent ethic, practices that would have been prophetic to the wider society and to the empire, the willingness to take on Rome directly seems to have varied. New Testament texts, such as 1 Peter 2:13–17, that call for submission to the emperor suggest that at least some of the Christian communities, at least some of the time, adopted a conciliatory attitude toward Rome. Other texts such as Revelation 13, which portrays the Roman empire as a murdering beast, reveal a hostile prophetic critique of

---

3. Yoder counts three incidents of mass nonviolent resistance by Judeans in Palestine between 26 CE and 50 CE. See, *Politics of Jesus*, 89–92.

the empire. Revelation portrays Christ and the church confronting and defeating the empire through prophetic word and martyrdom. The "powers and principalities" texts, such as 1 Corinthians 15:24; Ephesians 1:21; 6:12; and Colossians 2:15 that speak of God's clash with the powers and authorities of this world,[4] also reveal a strong confrontational posture for many of the early church communities. John's gospel, as will be shown, gives evidence that the Johannine community was one of these resistance churches.

VIEWS OF TORAH

The rabbinical community's new focus on and veneration of the Torah, with its consequent nonresistant posture, seems to have resulted in a counterargument from the Johanine community based on its view of Torah. While the rabbinical community emphasized the written Torah, the first five books of the Hebrew Scriptures, and its parallel oral Torah (eventually written down as the Mishnah), with numerous debates over the details of the teachings in these texts (these debates eventually forming the Talmud), the Johannine community drew on the tradition of a more expansive view of Torah for its message, and then focused this idea into the person of Jesus so that Torah became a very particular narrative idea.[5]

Already within Judaism there existed a more expansive view of Torah. Torah was sometimes equated with the Wisdom of

---

4. Walter Wink, in his *Powers* trilogy, has convincingly shown that the "powers and authorities" language of the New Testament refers both to earthly and heavenly powers and authorities that are mirrors of each other and that, in their fallen state, are in rebellion against God. In this light, much of the rhetoric of the New Testament can be understood to encourage followers of Christ to remain in the struggle with God against the powers and authorities who oppress the people and destroy the earth.

5. Rabbinic Judaism in no way denied the more expansive view of Torah, it merely did not seem to emphasize it during this period in the same way as the Johanine community did.

God.[6] The wisdom tradition within Judaism represented a major expansion of Torah in that Wisdom was sometimes understood as Torah for the nations. And indeed the prophets spoke of Torah going out to the nations (Isa 2:3). The identification of Torah with Wisdom gave Torah a more universal scope. It also gave Torah a pre-existence to its written form and to the world since, as mentioned above, Wisdom was understood to be present at the creation of the world.

The Hebrew Scriptures also spoke of Torah as the Word of God. For example, in Isaiah 2:3 Torah and the Word of God are in parallel and both go out from Jerusalem to the nations. But of course the Word of God involved more than Torah; it included the rest of the Hebrew Scriptures as well as any message that God gave to people such as when the word of God came to prophets. The same sort of argument might be made for Wisdom, and, as shown above, the concepts of Wisdom and Word of God overlapped and were often thought of as the same thing. So one might say that Torah was understood to participate in the Word and Wisdom of God, and by participating in the Word and Wisdom of God, could be conceptualized as expanding beyond its Israelite form and able to go out to the nations in a contextualized mode.

Torah's universal and timeless dimensions were embedded in the very concept of "Torah." The word "Torah" can be translated "law" or "instruction," and Torah was definitely both law and instruction. In the land of Israel, when the Israelites were autonomous, Torah was the law of the land. But it also contained their national stories and history and instructed them about who they were. When Israel was dominated by another power or expelled from the land, the instruction aspect of Torah became even more relevant for a people unable to practice the laws the way they could when they were free and in the land. So when Israel was virtually

6. Sirach is widely understood to promote this idea (see especially, 19:20 and 24:22–23), but other texts, including Baruch 3:9—4:4 and certain rabbinical texts, also make the equation between Torah and Wisdom. See the discussion in Sinott, *The Personification of Wisdom*, 135.

destroyed in 70 CE, the "instruction" and "wisdom" concepts of Torah, its more universal and timeless dimensions, became more relevant. It is this idea of Torah that the early church, especially the Johannine community, seized upon to craft its message.

JESUS AS TORAH

With this expansive view of Torah in mind, the Gospel of John presents Jesus as the Word of God and the Wisdom of God. This presentation implies that Jesus encompasses Torah as well, but the text provides us more than just this mere implication. What the narrator says about Jesus and what Jesus says about himself also point to Jesus as Torah: 1) Jesus is presented as the giver of Truth (1:17) and Truth itself (14:6); 2) Jesus is presented as the prophet-like Moses who gives himself to the people; 3) He is the source of living water, a symbol of Torah.

The text presents Jesus as greater than Moses (e.g., 1:17) but also as the prophet-like-Moses foretold in Deuteronomy 18:15–22. Whereas Moses gave the people the law, Jesus gives the people himself, since he himself is the Word of God and the Wisdom of God and the Truth (14:6); he becomes Torah for the people.

This presentation can be seen most clearly in chapter 6 where Jesus feeds the 5,000 and then offers them himself as the "bread of life." The feeding hearkens back to the miracle in the wilderness when God provided manna for Israel; in fact the imagery of this chapter signals a reenactment of the exodus event (more will be said about this new exodus later). Jesus plays the part of Moses, and the Torah that he gives is himself as "the bread of life." Jesus' imitation of Lady Wisdom becomes more pronounced in this passage. Lady Wisdom invites people to eat her bread and drink her wine just as Jesus does here. The heightening of Jesus' Wisdom persona makes clear the portrait of Jesus-as-Moses giving himself as Wisdom/Torah to the people. This portrait is strengthened by the people recalling Moses and the manna in the desert (6:31). It is also strengthened in that it is introduced by Jesus' exclamation at the very end of chapter 5 that Moses wrote about him.

Another clue that Jesus is Torah is found in Jesus' proclamation that he is the source of living water (4:10–14; 7:37–39). The text in 7:39 states that water symbolizes the Spirit, but this identification of water as a symbol for the Spirit seems to be a literary device to transfer Torah to Jesus and the Spirit that comes from him. Water in the Hebrew Scriptures often symbolized Wisdom or Torah (Prov 13:14; 18:4; Isa 55:1; Sir 24:21–29; 1 Enoch 48:1; 49:1) as well as the Spirit (Isa 32:15; 44:3–5). The rabbis also used water as a symbol for Torah.[7]

A TORAH MORE POWERFUL

By presenting Jesus as the Word of God, The Wisdom of God, the Truth and the Torah, the Johannine community argues that it has something greater and more dynamic than the mere written and oral Torah of the rabbinic community. It offers would-be believers from the synagogue a Torah that is bigger, more ancient and eternal, and more powerful. This Torah will not make peace with the beast of Rome. This Torah is the Torah of the cross that triumphs over Rome. John presents the way of the cross as the way to defeat Rome and its father, the devil.

The Torah of the Johannine community is a Torah whose wisdom is the way of the cross. Just as Lady Wisdom says, "they will seek me diligently, but will not find me" (Prov 1:28), Jesus, speaking of going to the cross, states, "You will search for me but you will not find me" (John 7:34). Jesus as Torah proclaims the secret wisdom of the cross, a wisdom that the powerful and the worldly cannot understand, a subversive wisdom that brings down empires.

---

7. E.g., Baba Kama 82a. Additionally, Brown, *John I – XII* 178, finds a mention of "living water" to refer to Torah in the Damascus Document.

This view of Jesus as Torah illuminates the arguments that Jesus has with the Judean leaders over his alleged breaking of the law. In these arguments, Jesus accuses them of having too narrow a view of Torah and accuses them also of breaking their own law. He states that their Torah, the one that Moses gave them, points to him, and that if they would actually listen to Torah, to the Wisdom of God, they would understand what he is doing.

Jesus as Torah also provides a Torah more adaptable outside the land of Palestine and after the destruction of Israel. By focusing on "wisdom" and creating a transnational new Israel, rather than redoubling efforts on how to apply laws meant for a certain time and place that exists no more, the Johannine community can recreate the community of God's people that can spread throughout the world and reach the gentiles, the people of the nations/kingdoms of this world.

6

The New Exodus

ONE OF THE LITERARY THEMES THAT UNDERGIRDS THE IDEA of resistance to Rome in the Gospel of John is that of a new exodus. The author of the Fourth Gospel presents Jesus as a new Moses, leading Israel out from under the domination of an imperial power. Just as Moses led the Israelites out of Egypt, so Jesus leads his followers to liberation from the Roman Empire, although Jesus does so, not by removing them from the empire, but by creating with them alternative communities within the empire.

The difference in the two exoduses is not that the first was political/national liberation and that the second is a mere "spiritual" liberation (such a dichotomy is a modern idea and would be anachronistic in the ancient world), but rather that while Moses led his people literally out of Egypt, Jesus leads his people to defect from the empire while still living in it. The reason for this strategy in the second exodus is not merely that leading the people out of the empire would be virtually impossible (where would they go? how would everyone be gathered from throughout the empire to make this journey?), but also because this exodus is to be ultimately less nationalistic than the first. While the new entity being created, the kingdom of God, is Israel reborn, it is to be a new transnational Israel, an Israel that takes in the gentiles and makes adjustments in its Torah to accommodate them.

One way of understanding this new entity is that, in its rebirth, Israel is to be transformed into the transnational kingdom of God, and this kingdom of God is to exist clandestinely in the kingdoms of this world, defecting from them, subverting them, and finally conquering them (16:33). This kingdom is to be in the world but not of it (17:6–26).[1]

JESUS AS MOSES

Toward the end of the prologue, the text declares, "The Law came through Moses, grace and truth came through Jesus the Messiah" (1:17). This pronouncement does not merely juxtapose Jesus with Moses, rather it sets forth Jesus as a second, even greater, liberator. The title *messiah* denoted a liberator figure who would come and deliver the people from their oppressors. Moses liberated the people when they were slaves in Egypt. Jesus would now liberate them in the context of the Roman Empire.

The Fourth Gospel will show Jesus to be like Moses, but even more so. In his conversation with Nicodemus, Jesus states that he

1. The term "world" (*kosmos*) seems to have a sociopolitical meaning in the NT, referring to the sociopolitical world that is hostile to, and in rebellion against, God and God's kingdom; the NT view holds that the kingdoms of this world have rebelled against the kingdom of God. The particular "kingdom of this world" in which the early church found itself was the Roman Empire, so the author of Revelation (a book widely recognized to be written specifically addressing the oppression of the church by Rome) refers to the Roman Empire as "the kingdom of this world" (11:15). Although the NT writers recognized that the "world" encompassed more than the Roman Empire, and that the same spirit of violence and domination active within the empire also operated in the world beyond the Roman Empire, their immediate context was the Roman Empire, so the term "world" (*kosmos*) often refers to the realities of that empire. Therefore, when Jesus says, in the language of realized eschatology, that he has "overcome the world" (John 16:33), he at once refers to the immediate context of the Roman Empire as well as to the world beyond. Walter Wink provides a helpful discussion of the term *kosmos* in *Engaging the Powers*, 51–59.

will give the same sign as Moses did in the desert when Moses lifted up a snake on a pole, but Jesus will not only give the sign, he will *be* the sign (3:14). In chapter 6, Jesus will feed the people as they were fed under the leadership of Moses when they received manna from God, but Jesus will both feed them bread and then offer them himself as food (6:1–15, 26–35). Later in the gospel, Jesus, in Moses-like fashion, gives commandments to his followers (13:34; 14:15, 21; 15:12). But whereas Moses gave the Torah, Jesus not only gives the sort of commandments that sum up the Torah, he also gives them *the* truth, a truth that will set them free (8:32), and is in fact himself the truth (14:6).

The passage in 8:31–38 provides us with a revealing scene that can help us understand the situation that the Fourth Gospel seems to be addressing. This passage references both the historical enslavement of the Hebrew people in Egypt and the contemporary occupation and oppression of Israel by the Romans. When Jesus tells his audience that the truth that he gives them can "make them free" (8:32), they respond "We are descendants of Abraham and have never been slaves to anyone" (8:33). The reader of the text should be immediately struck by the incredible denial by these people of both a central part of their historical narrative, which tells of their slavery in Egypt, and the current situation, in which they find themselves under Roman domination. This attitude of denial likely reflects the attitude of some of the rabbinic community in Asia Minor whom this text addresses. In the passage, Jesus responds to them by implying that they are slaves to sin. If they cannot see their current situation, and even deny their history, then they are slaves to the sin of this blindness (something that he addresses in the very next chapter). The point of the passage is that through truth-telling, Jesus liberates them from their bondage, political and spiritual, in the Roman system.

PASSOVER

Probably the major literary cue that points to the new exodus in John is the Passover theme—a theme that recalls the act of God that delivered the Hebrews from the Egyptian empire. The gospel narrative contains three episodes of Passover and presents Jesus as the Passover lamb.

The first two Passover occurrences foreshadow the crucifixion of Jesus, and the third tells the story of the crucifixion. At the first Passover, in 2:13–25, Jesus speaks of his death and resurrection, saying "destroy this temple and in three days I will raise it up." Next, in John 6, the text states the Passover is near, and Jesus invites his hearers to eat his flesh as bread and drink his blood as wine, an allusion to the Eucharist which symbolizes his sacrificial death. The third Passover occurs the week of the crucifixion.

The author presents Jesus as the Passover lamb, not merely by pairing the Passover occurrences with the crucifixion theme but also by having the Baptist introduce Jesus as "the Lamb of God" and by describing Jesus at the crucifixion as a Passover lamb. The passion narrative contains three clues that Jesus is the Passover lamb: 1) Jesus' death sentence comes at noon on "the day of preparation for the Passover" (19:14–16), which Raymond Brown points out is the time that the priests began slaughtering the lambs for Passover.[2] 2) When on the cross, he is given wine via a sponge on the end of a branch of hyssop that has been dipped in wine (19:29). Exodus 12:22 instructs those observing Passover to dip hyssop in the blood of the lamb to put it on the doorposts. As noted above, wine symbolizes the blood of Jesus, so symbolically speaking the hyssop at the crucifixion is dipped in the lamb's blood. 3) The text makes a point of saying that none

---

2. Brown, *John XIII–XXI*, 883, 895. See Exod 12:5–14; Brown states that by Jesus' time, the lambs were slaughtered by the temple priests, so they could not wait until twilight, as the Exodus passage actually instructs them to, because they had to slaughter enough lambs for 100,000 people. To address this problem, they interpreted twilight as being anytime after noon.

of Jesus' bones are broken and that this detail fulfills scripture (19:31–36). The scriptures regarding the preparation of Passover lambs, Exodus 12:46 and Numbers 19:12, instruct the preparers not to break any of the bones of the lamb.

While this portrayal of Jesus as the Passover lamb might seem to suggest to the modern reader a role for Jesus as a substitutionary sacrifice for individual souls, a decidedly non-sociopolitical salvation, the literary context of the times in which the text was written suggests otherwise. The image of a lamb in the first and second-century Jewish and Christian apocalyptic literature was often that of a *conquering* lamb. Revelation, a work contemporary with the Fourth Gospel, portrays Jesus as a "slain" lamb who "conquers" the Roman Empire. This idea of a lamb that is both "slain" and that "conquers" jibes well with the narrative of the Gospel of John which depicts the cross as the moment of Jesus' victory and in which Jesus says that he has "conquered the world" (16:33). Jesus as a slain Passover lamb is Jesus on the cross, victorious over his enemies. It is the idea that prophetic martyrdom (followed by resurrection) ultimately defeats the murderous forces of violence and domination. Jesus as the Passover lamb is the conquering lamb, leading his people out from under bondage to empire. In leading his people, Jesus calls them to follow in the way of the cross, to participate in this method of "conquering" the world. He never suggests, in John, that he is their substitute, rather he calls them to follow in the way of the cross. His call is participatory, not substitutionary.

THE MIDDLE PASSOVER

The second Passover occurrence, in John 6, has been called the exodus passage of the Fourth Gospel. The passage begins with Jesus performing a food miracle, feeding the people in a way that recalls God's provision of manna in the wilderness. The people begin to say that Jesus must be "the prophet," meaning the prophet-like

Moses foretold in Deut 18:15–18.[3] Later in the chapter, the people explicitly recall the manna miracle of the exodus (6:31).

The crossing of the "sea" in verses 16–21, by Jesus and his disciples reenacts the crossing of the Red/Reed Sea in Exodus. The disciples get into a boat to cross the "sea." (The next day the crowds would also get into boats to cross over.) They encounter strong winds, but after Jesus joins them, they immediately reach their destination. This scene seems to follow the exodus motif in Psalm 107 which, after proclaiming that God feeds the people who are hungry and have been wandering in the wilderness (verses 4–9), goes on to proclaim:

> Some went down to the sea in ships, doing business in the mighty waters.
> They saw the deeds of the Lord, his wondrous works in the deep.
> For he commanded and raised the strong wind, which lifted the waves of the sea.
> They mounted up to heaven, they went down to the depths.
> Their courage melted away in their calamity . . .
> He made the storm still . . .
> He brought them to their desired haven (23–30, NRSV).[4]

The use of the term "sea" (*thalassa*) also serves to cue the reader that this passage reenacts the Red/Reed Sea crossing. Outside the gospels, this body of water is referred to as a lake, both because of its small size and fresh water and because there is an actual sea nearby, the Mediterranean Sea. Howard-Brook notes that "the image of sea is mentioned 289 times in the Hebrew Scriptures, almost always in reference to the primal sea of crossing, the Red (Reed) Sea, the transversal of which marked the exodus journey in Exodus 11."[5]

---

3. See Brown, *John I–XII*, 49, 234.

4. Brown discusses a whole complex of scriptures and readings for Passover that support the idea that this passage reenacts the Red/Reed Sea crossing in *John I–XII*, 225.

5. Howard-Brook, *Becoming Children*, 142.

Only John calls this body of water "the Sea of Galilee of Tiberius." Tiberius was the emperor during Jesus' adult life time. Referring to this lake by that name speaks to the imperial context. This passage recalls the original exodus from the Egyptian empire and also references the current empire from which Jesus leads his people in a new exodus. The forces against them are as strong winds, but Jesus comes and immediately they prevail and reach their destination.

Jesus leads them across the imperial sea from the place of the feeding to the place where he can feed them his new wisdom, the word that can deliver them from the empire and all oppression and domination.

On the other side he invites them metaphorically into the way of the cross, into the prophetic martyrdom by which he will "overcome the world." He invites them to eat his flesh like bread and drink his blood like wine.

THE OTHER FESTIVALS

The two other festivals in John that are named (one is unnamed), the Festival of Tabernacles and the Festival of Dedication, also participate in the exodus theme of John. The Festival of Tabernacles, while also being a harvest festival, commemorated Israel's sojourn in the wilderness following its exodus from Egypt. The people constructed "tabernacles" or huts of the sort that the Israelites lived in while in the wilderness.

The Festival of Dedication did not commemorate an event associated with the exodus from Egypt, but did celebrate an event associated with the liberation from another empire. It commemorated the rededication of the temple after the Maccabean revolt liberated Israel from the domination of the Seleucid Empire.

John's narrative, through these festivals and other imagery, draws deeply from the traditions and history of Israelite liberation from imperial domination.

7

Wisdom's Assault
Everything You Know is Wrong

O NE WAY TO CONCEPTUALIZE THE PLOT IN THE GOSPEL OF John is to follow Jesus, as Wisdom, in his increasing assault on the worldly powers and authorities. As mentioned earlier, Jesus walks and talks like Lady Wisdom of the Hebrew Scriptures; in John, Jesus is Wisdom personified. As Wisdom he increasingly goes on the offensive, especially against the temple establishment, those who should understand Wisdom. In doing so, he eventually exposes their fear of worldly powers rather than God and reveals the temple establishment for the puppet government of the Roman Empire that it is.

In his assault, Jesus, as Wisdom, continually speaks and acts in ways that mystify his opponents, his disciples, and even the reader. His language is cryptic, his message inverts standard perceptions of reality, and he behaves as if it were Opposite Day, doing things the opposite of what one would expect him to do.

With his powerful words, Jesus, the Word/Wisdom of God, stops his adversaries from being able to arrest or execute him. This pattern repeats itself right up until and including his actual arrest. In that dramatic scene, his words demonstrate one last time that the arresting party has no power over him. His words cause them to fall to the ground.

Jesus' wisdom reveals itself to be a deceptively powerful trickster wisdom. It subverts the established order and drives out the "Ruler of this World" (12:31). In the persona of Lady Wisdom, Jesus says and does outrageous things that bewilder everyone and turn the world on its head.

OPENING SALVOS AND CRYPTIC LANGUAGE

Chapters 2–6 have Jesus going on the offensive with a temple cleansing and a healing, as well as crossing cultural boundaries with regard to sex and nationality to reach the Samaritans. All the while, he speaks in cryptic wisdom language that his opponents cannot understand. Twice, this cryptic wisdom-speak seems to keep his opponents at bay.

Jesus begins his public ministry with an actual physical assault on the temple establishment, or at least on the property of the merchants and money changers in the temple who work for the temple establishment (2:13–22). The author uses the same Greek word to describe Jesus "casting out" the employees of the temple establishment (2:15) as he does much later, in 12:31, to speak of "the Ruler of this world" being "cast out." Through this very physical temple cleansing, Jesus-as-Wisdom spiritually cleanses the temple by "casting out" the spirits of domination and exploitation.

Not only does such a highly aggressive act constitute pretty much the opposite of how a peasant rabbi might want to begin a public ministry (the other gospels put this story toward the end of his ministry, not the beginning), but it should surprise the reader because the previous story showed him hesitating to do anything publicly that might bring attention to himself and telling his mother that his "hour" has not yet come (2:4). This "hour" literally refers to the hour of his crucifixion.[1] The act of cleansing

---

1. 7:30; 8:20; 12:23; 12:27; 13:1; 16:32; 17:1.

the temple would not only bring Jesus plenty of attention, but it is also precisely the type of act that might quickly bring about his "hour." In Mark and Luke, we are told explicitly that the authorities react to the cleansing of the temple by seeking to "kill" Jesus (Mark 11:18; Luke 19:47). In John, interestingly, the reaction of the "Judeans" is more moderate, possibly because Jesus responds with cryptic wisdom about the destruction of the temple and his own resurrection. If his response is what keeps his adversaries at bay, then here we have the beginning of a pattern, throughout the story, of Jesus' words/wisdom stopping his enemies in their tracks.

When the Judeans demand a sign to prove his authority to cleanse the temple, he cryptically refers to himself as the temple, speaking of his crucifixion and resurrection: "'Destroy this temple, and I will raise it up in three days' . . . he was speaking of the temple of his body" (2:18–21). When Jesus identifies himself as the temple, the reader is reminded of the declaration in the prologue that Jesus, the word of God, "tabernacled among us" (1:14), a reference to Wisdom (Sir 24:8). The Judeans do not understand him, beginning a series of incidents in which Jesus' Judean opponents cannot understand Wisdom.

Astoundingly, after his assault on the temple establishment, no more real conflict occurs for a couple of chapters, but Jesus does continue to speak cryptically, in a way that inverts standard perceptions of reality, and he acts in ways contrary to culture. In speaking with Nicodemus, he again refers to his crucifixion, the result of his clash with the powers, but mentions no clash and refers to the crucifixion as his exaltation, inverting standard perceptions of reality with his words. Here we have the first of his three "lifted up" statements (3:14).

He then goes on to talk with and receive water from a Samaritan woman, a shocking crossing of ethnic and sexual boundaries in the context of ancient Semitic cultures. He also makes disciples of her and her people before he has gotten very far with his own people (4:1–41).

SUBVERSIVE WISDOM

The next conflict with the authorities occurs on his second trip to Jerusalem. He heals a lame man on the Sabbath. The Judeans respond not with wonder and thanksgiving but by "persecuting" Jesus (5:16). The response to the healing is stronger than the response to the physical assault at the temple. When they hear Jesus refer to God as his father, even though he made the same reference in his assault at the temple (2:16), the anger of the Judeans escalates, and we read for the first time that they want to kill him (5:18). Jesus responds by launching into a Wisdom-like first-person discourse, making outrageous claims about his identity and his life-giving work (compare John 5:24 with Prov 4:10–11, 20–22).

The scene ends abruptly after this speech. If his enemies were seeking to kill him then and there, Jesus' speech apparently stops them from being able to do so. In any case, it seems to keep his enemies at bay with Jesus getting the last word.

In chapter 6, Jesus feeds the multitudes in the wilderness and gives a long cryptic speech declaring that he is the "bread of life" and inviting people to "eat my flesh and drink my blood," words, as pointed out earlier, that echo Lady Wisdom (see Prov 1:20–21; 8:1–4; 9:3) and that prove too difficult for many of his disciples, causing them to leave him. Thus these first six chapters end with another act that seems counterintuitive for someone trying to build a movement; he alienates his own supporters via his cryptic Wisdom-speak.

CAT AND MOUSE

Chapters 7–10 intensify the conflict as the authorities start to actually send out the police to apprehend Jesus. He continually eludes them without having to leave Jerusalem, departing from the city only in his own time. In these scenes, Jesus' Wisdom-speak very clearly stops his enemies in their tracks.

Jesus begins this section by laying low in Galilee because the Judeans want to kill him. He tells his brothers that he will not go up to Jerusalem for the Festival of Tabernacles because his "time has not yet come" (7:6), but then he goes up "in secret" (7:1–10). Despite having gone up only "in secret," he begins teaching in the temple (7:14). By the end of the festival, he cries out his message (7:37), an act that reminds the reader of his Wisdom persona (see Prov 1:20; 8:1–4).

The temple establishment sends the police to arrest him, but he speaks to the police in the language of wisdom, saying that in a little while he is going away and they can search for him but will not find him and they cannot come where he is (7:33–34; compare with Prov 1:28–29). These words of wisdom stop the police from being able to arrest him; when the Sanhedrin questions the police as to why they did not arrest Jesus, they exclaim, "No one has ever spoken like that!" (7:45–46). We again see the amazing power of Wisdom to subvert the powers.

Throughout this section Jesus confuses the crowds, the police, and the Sanhedrin. The people begin arguing among themselves about who he is and where he is from (7:11–13, 25–27, 41–43). The members of the Sanhedrin and the police argue with each other (7:45–52). And no one is able to arrest him or stone him (7:30, 45–46; 8:20; 9:59; 10:39). As they repeatedly attempt to capture and kill him, he plays cat and mouse with them, all the while pointing out to them their inconsistencies, revealing to them their murderous intent (7:19–24; 8:44) and speaking of his death as his exaltation (8:28), the irony of which is lost on the crowds. Through actions and words, Jesus turns everything around. The crowds, the police, and the government are powerless against the outrageous words of this simple Galilean.

In the spirit of turning everything on its head, the text goes out of its way to tell us that the only person to embrace Jesus as "Lord" and "Son of Man" during this visit to Jerusalem is a blind beggar, someone at the very bottom of the social strata. He is the one who can "see," while the educated Pharisees remain "blind" (9:1–41).

THE FINAL CAMPAIGN

Jesus finally leaves Judea (10:40), only to return a short time later to launch one final assault against the temple establishment, the empire, and the forces of darkness that inhabit these institutional powers. In chapter 11, Jesus begins this final campaign against the powers with the simple, understated, almost absurd statement to his disciples, "Let's go to Judea again" (11:7). The statement is absurd not just because the authorities in Judea are actively trying to kill Jesus but because he has lingered for two days, knowing that his friend Lazarus would die as a result of the wait. After two days, he says, "Let's go to Judea again" then "Our friend Lazarus has fallen asleep, but I am going to wake him up" (11:11). We now begin to perceive a method to his madness. Jesus' final campaign against the powers of death and darkness will begin with a resurrection.

In between Jesus' two statements above, the disciples remind him that the Judean authorities are after him, and he responds in the language of light and darkness: "Are there not twelve hours of daylight? Those who walk in the day do not stumble because they see the light of this world. But those who walk at night stumble because the light is not in them." With this cryptic statement, he not only reveals the difference between his group—the twelve plus the Light of the World (see 8:12 and 9:5)—and his enemies who walk in darkness, he also foretells the event of his arrest in which his enemies come at night, with "lanterns and torches" because they have no light in them, and they "fall to the ground" (18:3–6).[2]

2. "Night" is part of the language of light and darkness in John, it is the time that the forces of darkness do their work. The coming night (9:4) is the night of Jesus' arrest and trial. Commenting on the arrest scene of 18:1–6, Brown notes, "In 13:27, 30, when we last saw Judas, he had become the tool of Satan and had gone off into the night. This was the evil night of which Jesus had warned in 11:10 and 12:35, the night in which men stumble because they have no light. Perhaps this is why Judas and his companions come bearing

This cryptic statement reveals that Jesus, in going to raise Lazarus back to life, intends for this journey to carry him to the cross. In other words, his invitation to his disciples to come on this journey is a call to wage war against the powers of death and darkness, beginning with the resurrection of Lazarus.

The resurrection of Lazarus proves to be the event that reveals the nature of the beast. The text has already spoken of the spiritual dimensions of Jesus' conflict with the authorities, in terms of light and darkness (1:5–9; 3:19–21; 5:35; 8:12; 9:4–5, 40–41; 11:9–10) and in terms of "the devil" as a "liar" and a "murderer" (8:44). Over and over this gospel has presented Jesus as the bringer of life (1:3–4; 3:15–16, 36; 4:14, 36; 5:24, 26, 40; 6:27–58, 63, 68; 8:12; 10:10, 28) and light (1:4–9; 3:19–21; 8:12; 9:5). Now, in this final assault on the powers, Jesus begins by bringing life in a concrete way, through raising someone from the dead back to life. This gift of life will prove to be the light that exposes the deeds of darkness. We have been told that the life that Jesus brings is light (1:3–4) and that this light exposes the deeds done in darkness (3:19–20). The ensuing conflict between Jesus and the authorities will illuminate the nature, the spirituality, of these institutional powers.

The first exposé of the powers comes right on the heels of the resurrection of Lazarus, in an amazingly revealing scene. The resurrection of Lazarus scares the Sanhedrin, leading it to convene a special session in which the fear of the empire rises to the fore: "What are we to do!? This man is doing many signs. If we let him go on like this, everyone will believe in him, and the Romans will come and take both our temple and our nation." In other words, upon hearing of this amazing sign of resurrection from God

---

lanterns and torches. They have not accepted the light of the world, and so they must have artificial light. This moment of darkness may be contrasted with the final triumph of Jesus in the heavenly Jerusalem (Rev 12:5) where the blessed will need no lamps for the Lord God will be their light. There is an echo of this same type of symbolism in the Lucan scene of the arrest (12:53) where Jesus says to his captors: 'This is your hour and the power of darkness'" (*John XIII–XXI*, 817).

through Jesus, the council immediately reveals that it fears the Roman Empire more than God (11:45–53). The council fears the powers of death more than the God of life.

The next passage (12:1–8) provides us with one of the most powerfully dramatic scenes of the story. After a brief retreat to the town of Ephraim, Jesus is back at the home of Martha, Mary, and Lazarus. Mary anoints Jesus' feet with expensive perfume and wipes them with her hair. In a culture where men and women keep their distance from each other outside of marriage, this sensual act would have been scandalous, but Jesus does not stop her, in fact he defends her bizarre behavior when she is criticized by Judas.

Aside from the touch between a man and a woman, another element of the scene that makes it so bizarre is that she anoints his *feet*. Interpreters have tried to make sense out of this detail without much success. Brown suggests that the feet might be anointed as part of the ritual to prepare a body for burial.[3] This interpretation fits well with Jesus' explanation that Mary is preparing him for burial, but Brown provides no citation.

The act of "anointing" itself has strong messianic and royal overtones. While anointing could be done for various purposes, the term "messiah" means "the anointed one," and anointing is strongly associated with kings in the Hebrew Scriptures (as well as with prophets, priests, and other people in special roles). The very next day, Jesus will be hailed as "King of Israel" (13:13). Mary seems to be anointing him, on a symbolic level, for his messianic kingly mission as well as for burial; in fact; in the upside down wisdom of this gospel, the two go together. He fulfills his role as Messiah and King through his death, when he is "lifted up." Usually, however, a king is anointed on his head, but the upside down wisdom of this gospel results in the anointing of the feet rather than the head. Not only is the symbolism upside down, but it foreshadows Jesus, having just entered Jerusalem hailed as "King of Israel," washing his disciples' feet in the very next chapter. This

3. Brown, *John I–XII*, 454.

"king" will act in the opposite manner that a king is supposed to act. The anointing of his feet, therefore, reflects this oppositeness, the upside down nature of his kingdom, a kingdom in which the greatest are called to be servants and to lay down their lives for each other (13:14; 15:12–17).

The next three verses show the response of the powers becoming even more violent. Despite the desperate efforts of the powers to stamp out resurrection, the joy and enthusiasm over this resurrection hope seems to be spreading out of their control. The Sanhedrin expands its hunt to include Lazarus as well as Jesus (12:9–11). They want to obliterate any sign of resurrection. Jesus counters by spoofing the powers.

The crowds wave Jesus into Jerusalem as a popular king, proclaiming him to be the "King of Israel." Jesus capitalizes on the moment to spoof the forces of empire: with no army and no weapons, he rides, not a war horse, but a donkey, a worker animal, as his royal means of transport in this enthronement ceremony. Jesus here engages in political theater, a parody of the grand military processional entrances of imperial dignitaries into important cities.[4] The dignitary would arrive with chariots and war horses in a display of grand imperial power. Jesus, in contrast, according to his upside down wisdom, rides a lone beast of burden, an animal of the people. Jesus' only weapons are his prophetic critique and resurrection hope, but these seem to be enough to overwhelm the powers. The Pharisees exclaim, "You see, you can do nothing, the world has gone after him!" (12:12–19).

This outburst of political street theater, that turns the imperial thought world on its head, leads to some of the most clearly articulated upside down wisdom of this entire gospel. Jesus proclaims

---

4. Recent interpreters have come to understand the events of Palm Sunday as political theater. See the discussions in Myers, *Strong Man*, 294–5, and Carter, *Matthew and the Margins*, 413–5. Some relevant ancient texts that speak of grand military processionals include: Josephus, *Antiquities* 11.325–39, 342–45 (regarding Alexander), Josephus, *Jewish Wars*, 4.112–20 (regarding Titus), and 1 Macc 13:51 (regarding Simon Maccabeus).

that "the hour" has come for him to be "glorified" (12:23), and then he proceeds to talk about his death. He speaks in parable as a sage. He describes the natural process by which death brings about life (12:24). He then goes on to the third and final of his "lifted up" statements (12:32). This time he not only describes the crucifixion as his exaltation but as the means by which he will "drive out" the "ruler of this world" (12:31). In other words, his march toward the cross is his march toward victory over the powers, his hour of "glory." The process by which the powers think they win, is the process by which they lose. Jesus' wisdom inverts worldly reality; it turns the world upside down.

Jesus then, as the newly foot-anointed king, acts like a king on Opposite Day. He washes his disciples feet, the job of a slave, not a king. He also teaches them to do the same for each other, for that is the way of this new heavenly kingdom that has come to earth to reverse the established order (13:1–20).

After these things, Jesus takes a break from his assault on the powers for the next four and one half chapters to teach, comfort, reassure, and pray for his new community.

Jesus re-enters the fray in chapter 18, going to a "garden" with his disciple where he knows they will be met by Judas with a detachment of soldiers and the police of the Sanhedrin. Peter acts according to the wisdom of this world and begins to fight back with a sword. Jesus rebukes him (18:1–11). Without recourse to the worldly wisdom of violence, Peter does not know what to do and winds up denying his association with Jesus just as Jesus had predicted earlier (14:36–38; 18:15–18, 25–27). He is unable to follow Jesus' reverse wisdom.

Having gone willingly into custody, Jesus faces interrogations by the high priest and then Pilate (18:19–24; 18:28—19:16). By the end of these interrogations, the chief priests and Pilate are all tied up in knots. Pilate is scared (19:8) and the chief priests, along with their police, are contradicting themselves: They both call for the release of a revolutionary insurgent and pledge their allegiance to

Caesar. Either one of these acts would normally be unthinkable. Revolutionaries attacked not only the Romans, but also the Judean elite, of which the high priests were the most elite. Also, even though the high priests where appointed by the Roman authorities and acted on their behalf, they would never admit so publicly by saying, "We have no king but Caesar!" Publicly, they were the leaders of Israel and their only king was God. To both call for the release of a revolutionary and pledge total allegiance to Caesar as their only king reveals just how confused and disordered they have become in trying to crush this trickster Messiah and stamp out the hope of resurrection.

Having exposed the fear of the powers and the temple establishment's complicity with Rome, Jesus allows himself to be crucified. The powers think they have won, but the reader knows that the true victor is Jesus.

Interestingly, the crucifixion scene in John lacks the dramatic apocalyptic aspects that are included in the crucifixion accounts of the other gospels. Mark and Luke record three hours of darkness and the rending of the temple curtain (Mark 15:33, 38; Luke 23:44–45). Matthew includes both of these events and adds an earthquake that causes a resurrection of saints (27:45, 51–53). Although John has made more of the crucifixion as the moment of Jesus' triumph than do the other Gospel narratives, John's version of the crucifixion omits the dramatic markers that signify the victory. John seems to rely more on the spoken wisdom of Jesus to emphasize the crucifixion as victory.

The resurrection of Jesus not only seals the victory of the cross, it constitutes the ultimate reversal of everything. Death, the final destiny of all people, has itself been reversed. The world has been turned on its head. The empire has been defeated. According to the wisdom of the world, the empire's power to dominate and kill should have assured its victory. The death of this upstart messiah should have been the end of the matter. The resurrection, however, reveals to the whole world, even the reader, that everything we know is wrong. The cross proves more powerful than the sword, and love conquers hate, so that even death is reversed.

8

Life After Jesus

THE JOHANNINE COMMUNITY LIVED AT A TIME SIXTY PLUS years after Jesus and twenty plus years after the destruction of the temple and, virtually, of Israel. They lived in a world that appeared completely subjugated to the powers of empire and domination. From all appearances, these dark powers seemed to have decisively won, and any attempts at resistance must have felt very difficult to contemplate.

The Johannine community experienced both oppression and marginalization and also the lure of accommodation that promised the possibility of improving their earthly lot. The oppression of Judeans, Christians, and other subjugated peoples in the Roman Empire of the first century is well attested, if sometimes exaggerated.[1] The temptation to accommodation, however, is less appreciated and usually understood only in terms of "religious" accommodation. Although the indignities and sufferings of oppression may have remained pervasive in their experience, Christians, Judeans, and other subjugated peoples throughout the empire, through accommodation, could experience varying degrees of privilege, or at least the easing of the yoke of oppression. They even sometimes achieved significant economic

1. See discussion in Carter, *John and Empire*, 68–72.

prosperity and respectability in the wider society by accommodating to the ways of "the world," an accommodation that could include participating in worship of the emperor.[2]

The Gospel of John calls a community in this context to active resistance to, even prophetic assault against, the powers and authorities of their world. It invites them into the way, the subversive wisdom, of the cross. It calls them to believe in the victory of the cross over the empire at time when all the evidence is to the contrary. Living at a time when the people of Israel have lost their temple and their homeland, they no longer have the physical manifestations of God's promises to hold on to. The empire seems to have completely won, and *its* gospel promises physical abundance.

In this time and context, the Gospel of John offers them Jesus who is the new temple and the embodiment of Israel. This gospel addresses their need . . . except that Jesus, too, is not physically with them; they have only the Spirit. In fact, Jesus has told them repeatedly that he must go so that the Spirit can come. And so the last two chapters of the gospel present the community with their hope—the risen Christ, the physical evidence of the promise of victory over the powers of this world—but they cannot "hold on" to him; he must ascend so that the Spirit will come and lead them to victory. They must learn to live in the Spirit, to see with spiritual eyes. (Interestingly, Jesus, in these last two chapters of John, never gets around to actually ascending. This peculiar characteristic of a narrative so focused on the ascension may reflect the anxiety of the community that produced this text as a message, in part, to itself.)

In these last two chapters, the disciple community has just experienced the loss of Jesus in the crucifixion. The empire, the "ruler of this world," appears to have won. Their experience, of course, mirrors the Israelite experience of losing temple and land. Into this faith-crushing trauma, the last two chapters of John announce the resurrection in a way that engages the context of the Johannine community with the following themes: 1) believing

2. Ibid., 26–45.

Life After Jesus

without seeing; 2) signs of victory in the present, including the preservation of the community; 3) a final invitation into the subversive wisdom of the cross.

THE EMPTY TOMB

Chapter 20 begins with the discovery of the empty tomb (1–9), which represents both the victory of the resurrection and the absence of Jesus. This passage sends us straight into the context of the Johannine community. The passage ends by saying that not until the beloved disciple, the representative of the Johannine community, sees the empty tomb does he believe and understand that Jesus has risen from the dead (8–9). The absence of Jesus, the empty tomb, becomes the source of faith! The Johannine community can easily find itself in this passage, having to believe, in the absence of Jesus, in the absence of land and temple and any of the physical manifestations of God's promises, having to believe in the way of Jesus when the way of the empire appears to be triumphant with plenty of physical manifestations of its victory. In this passage the Johannine community, embodied in the beloved disciple, believes on the basis of an empty tomb.

This passage also contains the theme of the call of the disciple community into the way of the cross. The beloved disciple reaches the tomb first and then Peter arrives and goes inside. Only after Peter has gone in does the beloved disciple enter the tomb. Tradition records that the beloved disciple was never martyred but died of natural consequences. The text of John tells us that the beloved disciple did not hesitate to follow Jesus to the cross as Peter did. The beloved disciple is the only one of the twelve that is recorded in John to be at the foot of the cross when Jesus is crucified (19:26–27). Peter, on the other hand, denies Jesus three times (18:15–18, 25–27). Tradition tells us, however, that Peter was eventually martyred upside down on a cross. So the beloved disciple followed Jesus to the cross first, but did not die; metaphorically he does not enter the tomb until much later, after Peter. Peter, on the other hand, fails to "follow" Jesus to the cross when Jesus in crucified, just as Jesus predicted, but he does "follow later." In 13:36–38, Jesus says to Peter "Where I am going, you cannot follow now, but you will follow later." In this first resurrection passage, Peter arrives at the tomb second, after the beloved disciple, symbolic of his hesitance to go to the cross. But he goes into the tomb first, symbolic of his martyrdom, his actual death, that occurs before the beloved disciple John.

The text states that Peter arrived at the tomb "following him and entered into the tomb" (20:6). Peter "follows" the beloved disciple, who followed Jesus, to the cross. Both disciples "follow" Jesus to the cross, but not at the same time, and only one dies on a cross, signaling that following Jesus in the way of the cross does not always involve literal martyrdom.

"DON'T HOLD ON TO ME"

The gospel could almost end with the empty tomb passage, or at least skip to Jesus' meeting with the disciples in 20:19–23 and end there, but the text pauses to tell the dramatic story of the meeting between Jesus and Mary Magdalene which emphasizes the need to let Jesus go. Jesus tells Mary, "Do not hold on to me because I have not yet ascended to the Father" (20:17).

Throughout the gospel, Jesus has been saying that he is going somewhere that his enemies cannot follow, by which, as explained above, he means that he is going to the cross and then back to God. Jesus works hard to reassure his disciples that his departure will be a good thing for them. He repeatedly describes the crucifixion as victory over the powers (e.g., 3:13; 8:28; 12:32). In chapter 14 he states that there are "many dwelling places" in his "father's house" and that he must go because he will "prepare a spot" for them and come back to take them to where he is ("where I am," 14:1–3). As chapter 14 unfolds, we find that the "dwelling place" being prepared is the community of disciples, i.e., the church. He states that he will send the "advocate," "the Spirit of Truth," to remain with them (15–17). He says,

> I will not leave you orphaned; I am coming to you. In a little while the world will not see me, but you will see me; because I live, you also will live. On that day you will know that I am in the Father, and you in me, and I in you. They who have my commandments . . . we will come to them and make our *dwelling place* with them . . . I am going away, and I am coming to you" (18–28).

Jesus must go so that, in triumphing over the powers, he can then come back in Spirit to build the church. His going prepares the way for the church to be born in the Spirit. Taking his followers to where he is begins with the Spirit's building of the church, whose members follow in the way of the cross to victory over the "ruler of this world." All of this can happen if they just let him go and continue to believe: "If you loved me, you would rejoice that I am going to the Father . . . I have told you this before it occurs, so that when it does occur, you may believe . . . for the ruler of this world is coming" (14:28–30).

Chapter 16 picks up this theme again, with emphasis on the victory over the "world" or the "ruler of this world" and, again, an overt mention of the difficulty of believing without seeing (a fairly overt reference to this dilemma occurred in 14:19, quoted above):

> It is to your advantage that I go away, for if I do not go away, the advocate will not come to you . . . and having come, it will expose the world concerning sin and justice and judgment: concerning sin, because they do not believe in me; concerning justice, because I am going to the Father and you will not see me any longer, concerning judgment because the ruler of this world has been condemned" (16:7–11).

Jesus must depart so that the Spirit can come and build the church and lead it to victory over "the ruler of this world." If Mary Magdalene holds on to him, he cannot come back to fulfill the plan.

SEEING, SENDING, BELIEVING

In the next two scenes, Jesus appears to his disciples who are gathered in a safe house. The first of these passages (20:19–23) could close the gospel. Jesus appears to his disciples, shows them his hands and his side, commissions them, and then imparts to them the Holy Spirit, giving them authority. The text could end there, maybe also adding the closing remarks in verses 30 and 31, but it adds another passage addressing the "seeing without believing" theme. Interestingly, in the initial passage in this section, Jesus shows the disciples his hands and his side with no special urging. His appearance as the crucified and risen Messiah seems to naturally call for this presentation: here he stands, the physical evidence that the way of the cross triumphs over the way of the world, and yet that is not the experience of the Johannine community. All the physical evidence around them points in the opposite direction. So the story of "doubting Thomas" is added to provide the community with the admonition, "Do not doubt but believe . . . blessed are those who have not seen and yet believe" (20:27–29).

The theme of believing without seeing is so strong in this section that we can easily miss the theme of commissioning in the first passage. Jesus shows his disciples his hands and his side, recalling the crucifixion, and then says, "As the Father has sent me, so I send you" (20:21). In other words, Jesus sends them on the journey that he has just been on; he sends them the way of the cross.

He then breathes on them the Holy Spirit and gives them authority to forgive sins. As described above in chapter 2, the power to forgive sins constitutes the legal authority to restore people to the community, to give them full social standing, and therefore access within a society. It seems to have been the most fundamental sociopolitical authority, for it is the one that is mentioned by the imperial propaganda as the authority of the emperor. By giving this authority to the disciples, Jesus declares victory over the world. This new community, this new nation, he declares, is even now the one that has dominion throughout the earth, despite all the evidence to the contrary. To see this reality, one must have the eyes of faith, one must believe without seeing.

A SECOND ENDING

The last two verses of chapter 20 read like a nice ending to the book, and maybe they were at some stage in the composition of the gospel. Chapter 21, however, continues to address the context of the Johannine community and, as in chapter 20, does so with themes and imagery from earlier in the gospel. Both chapters appear to be thematically interwoven with the rest of the text.

The text of chapter 21 begins by informing the reader that this next resurrection appearance by Jesus occurs by the lake of Galilee which is referred to as the "Sea of Tiberias," giving the scene an imperial context. The disciples fish through the night and catch nothing. Brown notes that nighttime fishing was common,[3] but the symbolism of night and day is also significant here. In John, night is the time when "no one can work" (9:4) and when people "stumble" (11:10) as opposed to the day (9:4; 11:9). Following this symbolism, the disciples catch nothing during the night, but then Jesus shows up in the morning and enables them to catch a large number of fish, specifically 153 fish.

Interpreters have puzzled at the number 153. Not only do ancient writers, including biblical writers, place major symbolic significance in numbers, but whereas this gospel tends to use fuzzy numbers (e.g., 1:39; 6:10; 21:8), here the text gets very specific: 153. This number must mean something! Brown surveys the range of meanings that interpreters have suggested for this number, everything from the supposed number of fish cataloged by Greek zoologists to various words and phrases whose numerical values (the sum of the numerical values of their letters) total 153. One theory that has not been suggested, however, is that 153 may be a number

3. Brown, *John XIII–XXI*, 1069.

related to the community of disciples, the church (one possibility might be the number of members of the Johannine community at the time this text was written). The reasons for this number representing the church are as follows: 1) The image of the fish, specifically the word *ichthys*, used when giving the number of fish caught, was an early Christian symbol representing individual Christians or the church collectively and may have been known by this time by the Johannine community;[4] 2) The wider Gospel tradition contains the idea of "catching fish" as building the church or "catching people" (Matt 4:19; Luke 5:4–7); 3) This story closely resembles the story in Luke 5:1–11, and in that story the nets are so full of fish that they begin to tear, whereas in the John version the net does not tear despite the great number of fish. John's version contains this critical difference that carries a theme from chapter 17, that Jesus has not lost any of those entrusted to him by God (17:12) and prays that God will continue to protect them after he leaves (17:6–26). The fish, then, are the disciples who are kept secure in God's net; the community will be preserved; 4) Paradoxically, along with the preservation of the community comes the call to walk in the way of the cross. Brown notes that the verb used for catching fish, *piazō*, used in verses 3 and 10, is not normally used for catching fish, and the other six times that it occurs in John, it is used of the arrest of or attempted arrest of Jesus[5] (the four other occurrences of the verb in the NT denote an arrest or capture as well: Acts 3:7; 12:4; 2 Col 1:32; and Rev 19:29); the implication here is that these fish are the disciples who follow in the way of Jesus and are all subject to arrest in the same way that Jesus was; being kept secure in God's net does not preclude arrest and martyrdom.

Regardless of the actual meaning of the number 153, two almost contradictory themes in this passage present themselves clearly: God's provision of abundant life and the call to the way of the cross. Once the disciples haul the large catch of fish ashore,

4. Hassett, "Symbolism."

5. Brown, *John XIII–XXI*, 1069.

Jesus feeds them a meal of fish and bread. This meal recalls the feeding of the five thousand in chapter 6, also a meal of fish and bread and also a miracle of abundant food provision. In chapter 6, the meal is followed by a discourse in which Jesus offers himself as bread and wine. This meal and discourse constitute the Eucharist in John (the actual last supper in John is not narrated as a Eucharist). Through this eucharistic discourse, Jesus invites the people into the way of the cross (see chapter 5). Since the meal in chapter 21 recalls that first eucharistic miracle feeding and discourse, it is also an invitation into the way of the cross. The narration in verse 13 of Jesus feeding them the meal has a eucharistic feel to it, with Jesus "taking" the first element of the meal and giving it to the disciples and then doing the same with the second (compare to 1 Cor 11:23-26). The meal constitutes both a sign of the abundance of God's reign and a call into the way of the cross.

THE REHABILITATION OF PETER AND THE FINAL CALL TO THE CROSS

This final passage (15-23) of the last two chapters of John brings the reader back to where these two chapters began, with Peter and the beloved disciple in a resurrection scene that speaks of their different journeys in the way of the cross. In this passage, Jesus rehabilitates Peter and affirms the way that both he and the beloved disciple "follow" him.

Just as Peter earlier denied Jesus three times, in this passage he declares his love for Jesus three times at Jesus' invitation. In rehabilitating Peter, Jesus uses words and imagery that are the language of the way of the cross, not only giving Peter a second chance at following him in the way of the cross, but referring to all who follow him as those who follow in the way of the cross.

After inviting Peter to declare his love for him, Jesus each time gives Peter the instruction to care for the disciple community. He says first "feed my lambs" (15), then "tend my sheep" (16), and then "feed my sheep" (17). The first instruction, "feed my lambs," uses the word for "lamb," *arnion*, that occurs twenty-nine times in Revelation to refer to Christ where Christ-as-lamb is introduced as "a lamb standing as if it had been slaughtered" (5:6), an image for the crucified Christ.[6] In the second two instructions, Jesus uses the word *probaton*, the word used in the ancient Greek version of the Hebrew Scriptures to refer to the Passover lamb. Just as Jesus has been portrayed in this gospel as a Passover lamb, he in turn refers here to his followers as Passover lambs. All three times, therefore, Jesus refers to those who follow after him as people following in the way of the cross.

The admonition to feed the sheep recalls the previous scene in which Jesus just fed the disciples in a eucharistic fashion, inviting the disciples into the way of the cross. Jesus uses two words, *boskō* and *poimainō*. Both words are used to translate the same verb from the Hebrew in the ancient Greek version of the Hebrew Scriptures, but *poimainō* has a wider range of meaning and can be translated either "feed" or "tend/shepherd." The intended meaning for *poimainō* in this passage may be both "tend/shepherd" and "feed" with the idea that Jesus is calling Peter to follow after him by being a shepherd (*poimainō* is the verbal form of a noun that means "shepherd") who "lays down his life for the sheep" (10:11). Both verbs, therefore, carry the theme of the cross.

Jesus then predicts Peter's arrest and execution and ends his prediction with the admonition, "follow me," using the same language he used when he predicted Peter's failure to follow him to the cross (13:36–38). Having been fully restored to the way by Jesus, Peter then asks about the beloved disciple, whom tradition

6. Revelation goes on to speak of Jesus sometimes as merely a "lamb" (e.g., 5:8) and sometimes as a "slaughtered lamb" (e.g., 5:12). The word used for "lamb" to refer to Jesus in John 1:29 and 36 is a different word, *amnos*, which is the word the Septuagint (the ancient Greek translation of the Hebrew Scriptures) uses in Exod 12:5 for the Passover lamb. Normally the Septuagint uses the word *probaton* for the Passover lamb, the other word used in this John passage.

says died of natural causes. Jesus affirms the discipleship of this disciple and repeats the admonition "follow me" (21:22), signaling that following in the way of the cross does not necessarily lead to actual martyrdom.

This gospel is written to a community that is tempted to accommodate to the way of the world because all of the physical evidence around them points to the apparent victory of that way. To counter all of that evidence, the narrative of this gospel provides them with a "heavenly" perspective; it tells the story of someone who subverts the wisdom of this world and opens their eyes to see that everything they know about reality is wrong: the strong do not always prevail over the weak, one's family of origin and place of birth do not determine one's destiny, and life can ultimately survive death. This gospel relentlessly invites the reader into the way of the cross as the way to abundant life. Its wisdom is counterintuitive and can only be understood when one is born of the Spirit.

Bibliography

Bauckham, Richard. *The Theology of the Book of Revelation*. New Testament Theology. Cambridge: Cambridge University Press, 1993.

Braund, David C. *Augustus to Nero: A Sourcebook on Roman History 31 BC–AD 68*. Totowa, NJ: Barnes & Noble, 1985.

Brown, Raymond. *The Gospel According to John I–XII*. Anchor Bible 29. New York: Doubleday, 1966.

Brown, Raymond. *The Gospel According to John XIII–XXI*. The Anchor Bible 29a. New York: Doubleday, 1966.

Carter, Warren. *John and Empire: Initial Explorations*. New York: T & T Clark, 2008.

———. *Matthew and the Margins: A Sociopolitical and Religious Reading*. The Bible and Liberation. Maryknoll: Orbis, 2000.

Cohen, Shaye J. D. *From the Maccabees to the Mishnah*. Library of Early Christianity. Philadelphia: Westminster, 1987.

Evans, Craig A., ed. *The Bible Knowledge Background Commentary*. Colorado Springs: David C. Cook, 2003.

Hanson, K. C., and Douglas E. Oakman. *Palestine in the Time of Jesus: Social Structures and Social Conflicts*. 2nd ed. Minneapolis: Fortress, 2008.

Hassett, Maurice. "Symbolism of the Fish." *The Catholic Encyclopedia* 6. New York: Robert Appleton, 1909. Online: http://www.newadvent.org/cathen/06083a.htm.

Horsley, Richard A. *The Liberation of Christmas: The Infancy Narratives in Social Context*. New York: Continuum, 1993.

Howard-Brook, Wes. *Becoming Children of God: John's Gospel and Radical Discipleship*. The Bible and Liberation. Maryknoll: Orbis, 1994.

Malina, Bruce J., and Richard L. Rohrbaugh. *Social-Science Commentary on the Synoptic Gospels*. Minneapolis: Fortress, 1992.

Myers, Ched. *Binding the Strong Man: A Political Reading of Mark's Story of Jesus*. Maryknoll: Orbis, 1988.

Nickelsburg, George W. E. "Son of Man." In *The Anchor Bible Dictionary* 6:137–50. New York: Doubleday, 1992.

Schwartz, Seth. *Imperialism and Jewish Society: 200 B. C. E. to 640 C. E.* Princeton: Princeton University Press, 2001.

Sinnott, Alice M. *The Personification of Wisdom.* Society for Old Testament Study Series. Burlington, VT: Ashgate, 2005.

Wink, Walter. *Engaging the Powers: Discernment and Resistance in a World of Domination.* Minneapolis: Fortress, 1992.

———. *Naming the Powers: The Language of Power in the New Testament.* Philadelphia: Fortress, 1984.

———. *Unmasking the Powers: The Invisible Forces that Determine Human Existence.* Philadelphia: Fortress, 1986.

Yoder, John Howard. *The Politics of Jesus.* 2nd ed. Grand Rapids: Eerdmans, 1972.